LIFE: A JOURNEY

THROUGH TIME

FRANS LANTING

EDITED BY
CHRISTINE ECKSTROM

TASCHEN

LEFT: Boulders and Surf, Hawaii
PREVIOUS PAGE 1: Petrified Wood, Arizona; PAGES 2–3: Volcano, Hawaii; PAGES 4–5: Moonrise, Wyoming;
PAGES 6–7: Stromatolites, Australia; PAGES 8–9: Moon Jellies, California; PAGES 10–11: Water Lilies, Botswana;
PAGES 12–13: Quiver Trees, South Africa; PAGES 14–15: Giant Tortoises, Galápagos Islands; PAGES 16–17: Marine
Iguanas and Brown Pelican, Galápagos Islands

One spring evening seven years ago I stood at the tide line of an estuary in the eastern United States watching something that took me far back in time. I saw horseshoe crabs come out of the water to spawn, an ancient ritual that goes back hundreds of millions of years. That experience made me realize that I could see the past in the present. And I wondered whether it might be possible to tell the story of life on Earth from its earliest beginnings to its present diversity by capturing images that evoke nature through time. That is how the idea for this book was born. Ever since that encounter with horseshoe crabs, I've been on a personal journey through time, looking for situations in the natural world that provide a window on its past.

I made pilgrimages to haunting time capsules like Shark Bay, a remote lagoon in Western Australia, where life-forms whose lineage goes back more than three billion years still dominate the landscape. I joined an expedition to a secluded valley of spewing geysers and hissing hot springs in Siberia's Kamchatka Penisula for a glimpse of the conditions that may have nurtured the birth of life itself. I immersed myself in museums and research collections to photograph the bewildering shapes of microscopic diatoms, the fluid geometries of oceanic jellies, and to visualize patterns inside the human body as parallels to patterns on the surface of the Earth. And I gained a new perspective on the snails that slide silently through my own backyard as echoes from an era when life was just crawling out of the sea.

Nature in most places appears as a chaotic mosaic of species that live together in the present but have their origins in different times. My challenge was to untangle nature from its entwinements in the present and represent the strands separately and chronologically. My goal was to create a sequence of images that can be viewed as slices through time. Out of necessity, this book presents a very selective interpretation of the history of life. My approach has been that of a storyteller who draws on characters for the sake of telling a larger tale. To weave my ideas together in a sequence that makes sense chronologically and thematically, I wrote a script, "A Journey Through Time," which summarizes the main events expressed by the photographs.

The book's first chapter, "Elements," interprets Earth's early history, before there was life, and consists of images that show interactions among the five classical elements originally recognized by Greek and Hindu philosophers: earth, air, fire, water, and space. "Beginnings" traces life from its single-celled origins through its evolution into more complex forms in the sea. "Out of the Sea" deals with the phase when life ventured ashore but was still dependent on water as a medium for reproduction. "On Land" covers the period when plants and animals succeeded in colonizing solid ground. "Into the Air" highlights the evolutionary innovations of birds and flowering plants, a chapter that ends with the cataclysmic events that caused the demise of dinosaurs and many other life-forms. "Out of the Dark" portrays the rise of mammals, and the concluding chapter, "Planet of Life," envisions the collective force of life as a sixth element that shapes our planet.

We are living in an extraordinary time: Our knowledge about life on Earth is growing rapidly through advances in scientific disciplines ranging from microbiology to paleontology, from geology to astrobiology. The integration of that knowledge is increasing our understanding about the interconnected nature of life, and the role it plays as a whole in influencing the conditions that make this planet hospitable to life. That realization has inspired my work.

This book is a synthesis of my career. I started out as a wildlife photographer pursuing animals one at a time. As I learned more about their lives, my view grew to include their habitats, and animals became ambassadors for ecosystems. Biodiversity superseded ecosystems as a concept for understanding nature as a network made up of untold numbers of species. Yet every one of those living organisms has a unique origin in time, and that is the dimension I have attempted to convey in this book. It is humbling to imagine the immensity of time covered by the history of life on Earth. But that is what I plunged into, with curiosity and wonder. And I emerged from this journey with a different sense of myself in time. *Life* follows in the wake of *Eye to Eye*, which expressed the kinship of all animal life, and *Jungles*, which explored the complexities of nature in the tropics. I hope this book will contribute to bridging the gap between a naturalist's appreciation for nature and a scientist's understanding of life. It is my tribute to the kinship and continuity of all life on Earth.

Frans Lanting
Santa Cruz, California

ELEMENTS

The journey of life starts in space, where energy becomes matter,

turning into shapes over time,

solidifying into spheres fueled by fire.

Once fire gives way, Earth emerges.

But this is an alien planet.

The Moon is closer. Things are different.

Heat within Earth makes volcanoes erupt, exhaling gases into the sky.

Geysers vent steam, and when Earth cools,

rain falls for eons, giving birth to oceans.

Water freezes around the Poles and shapes the edges of the Earth.

Water is a key to life, but in frozen form it is a latent force.

When water vanishes, Earth becomes like Mars.

But this planet is restless; it roils inside.

And where that energy touches water, a new element appears: Life.

BEGINNINGS

Life arises around cracks in the Earth.

Mud and minerals become substrates where life begins to multiply,

thickening in places, growing structures under a primeval sky.

Once single cells learn to capture sunlight, they alter the atmosphere,

creating a breath for all life thereafter.

A breath that became fossilized as iron.

Life needs a breath and it needs a membrane to contain itself,

so it can replicate and mutate.

Shallow seas nurture life early on, as it grows into more complex forms.

Life evolves when light and oxygen increase.

Life hardens and becomes defensive.

Life learns to move and begins to see.

The first eyes grow on trilobites.

OUT OF THE SEA

Vision is refined in horseshoe crabs, among the first to leave the sea.

They still do what they have done for ages, their enemies long gone.

Scorpions follow prey out of the sea, where slugs become snails.

Fish try amphibian life and frogs adapt to deserts.

Lichens develop as a co-op: Fungi marry algae.

They cling to rock and transform barren land.

True land plants arise, leafless at first.

Once they learn to stay upright, they grow in size and shape.

The fundamental forms of ferns follow, bearing spores that foreshadow seeds.

Life flourishes in swamps.

ON LAND

A great change rocks the Earth; continents get dry.

On land life turns tough; jaws form first, teeth come later.

Crocodiles and tuataras are echoes of that era.

It takes time for life to break away from water,

and it still beckons all the time.

With eggs and seeds life has a chance on land

to shelter new life in the making.

Life protects itself with scales and skin when it ventures inland;

some dragons from the past are still alive today.

Dinosaur time shimmers in parts of Madagascar and Brazil,

where plants like cycads remain rock hard

and others still grow defenses against foraging giants.

But as continents move, climates change.

Conifers adapt to cooling in times when Earth turns frigid.

INTO THE AIR

When Earth warms, green forests nurture things with wings.

One early form left an imprint like it fell only yesterday,

while others fly today like visions from the past.

In birds life gains new mobility.

Flamingos cover continents. Migrations get underway.

Birds witness the emergence of flowering plants:

Water lilies are among the first.

In Australia a lily turns into a grass tree;

in Hawaii a daisy becomes a silversword.

In ancient Gondwana drought molds proteas.

But when that great continent breaks up, life gets lush.

Jungles arise, sparking new layers of interdependence.

Fungi multiply.

Orchids emerge, their genitalia shaped to lure insects.

Coevolution entwines insects and birds with plants forever.

But when birds can't fly they become vulnerable.

Extinction can come slowly, but sometimes it happens fast.

When an asteroid hits the Earth, a world vanishes in flames.

But there are witnesses, survivors in the dark.

OUT OF THE DARK

When the skies clear, a new world is born, a world fit for mammals.

From tiny shrew-like creatures accustomed to the dark, new forms radiate:

Hyenas, lions, cheetahs, getting faster, and faster still.

Grasslands create opportunities, where safety comes from sharpened senses.

Growing big is another answer, but size often comes at a price.

Some mammals turn back to water:

Sea lions get sleek and adapt to cold with layers of fat;

whales and dolphins move into a world without bounds.

There are many ways to be a mammal.

Kangaroos hop in Australia, horses run in Asia,

and wolves stalk on stilt legs in Brazil.

Primates evolve in jungles; tarsiers first, lemurs not much later.

Learning becomes reinforced.

Bands of apes venture into the open when forests dry out once more.

Going upright becomes a lifestyle.

So who are we? Brothers of masculine chimps? Sisters of feminine bonobos?

We are all of them and more. We are molded by the same force.

The blood veins in our hands echo the course water traces on the Earth.

Our brains, our celebrated brains, reflect the drainage of a tidal marsh,

but they enable us to imagine a whole Earth.

PLANET OF LIFE

Life is a force in its own right.

It is a new element. It has altered the Earth.

Life covers Earth like a skin.

And where it does not, as in Greenland in winter,

the margins for life become clear.

But where water is liquid, it is a womb for cells green with chlorophyll,

and that molecular marvel has made the difference.

It fuels everything on Earth.

The animal world today lives on oxygen released by algae, bacteria, and plants:

Their waste is our breath; our exhalation is theirs.

This Earth is alive, and it has made its own membrane,

a biosphere made of land, sea, and air,

energized by all living things

forming a whole that is held together and sustained

by the collective power of life.

ELEMENTS

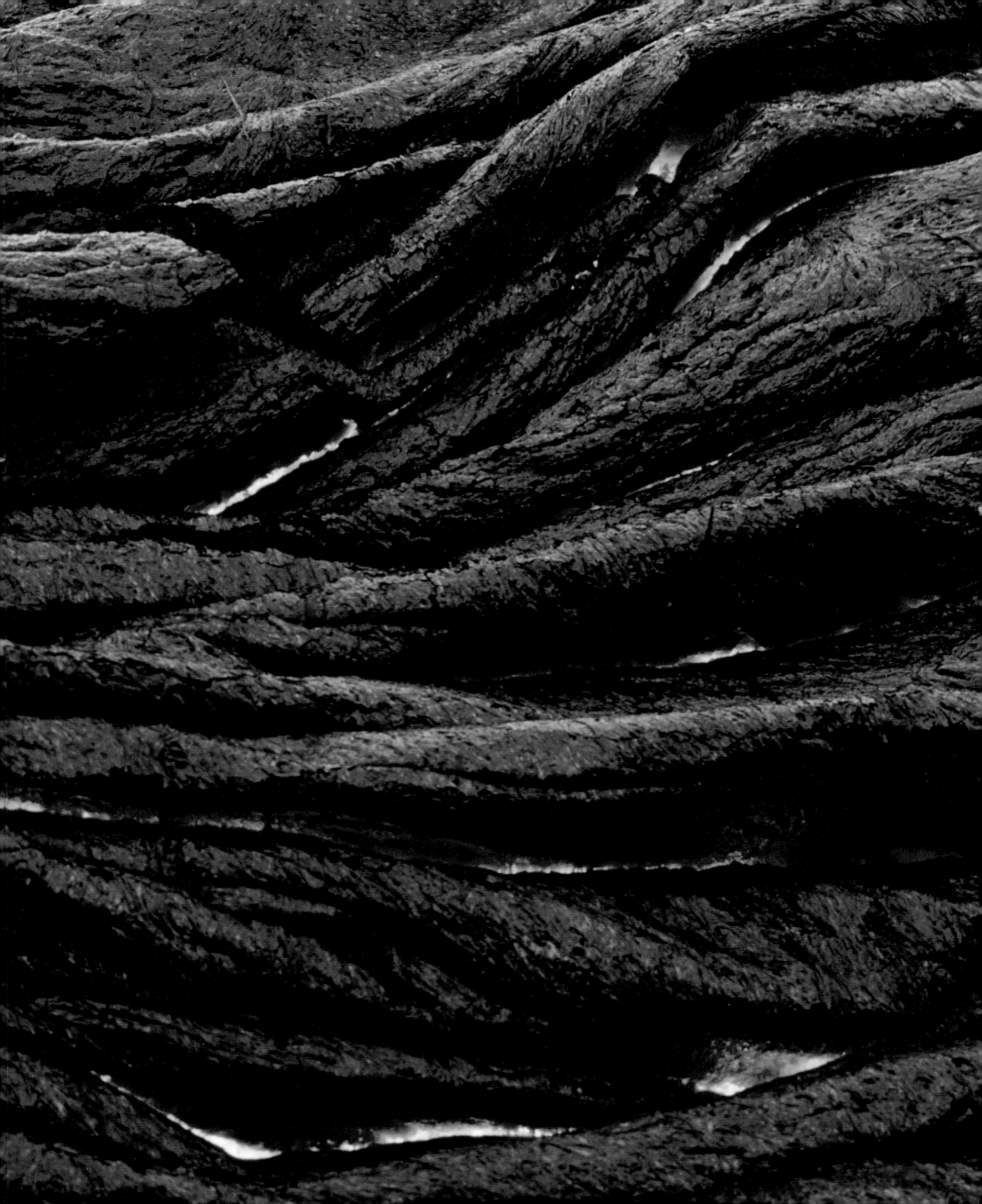

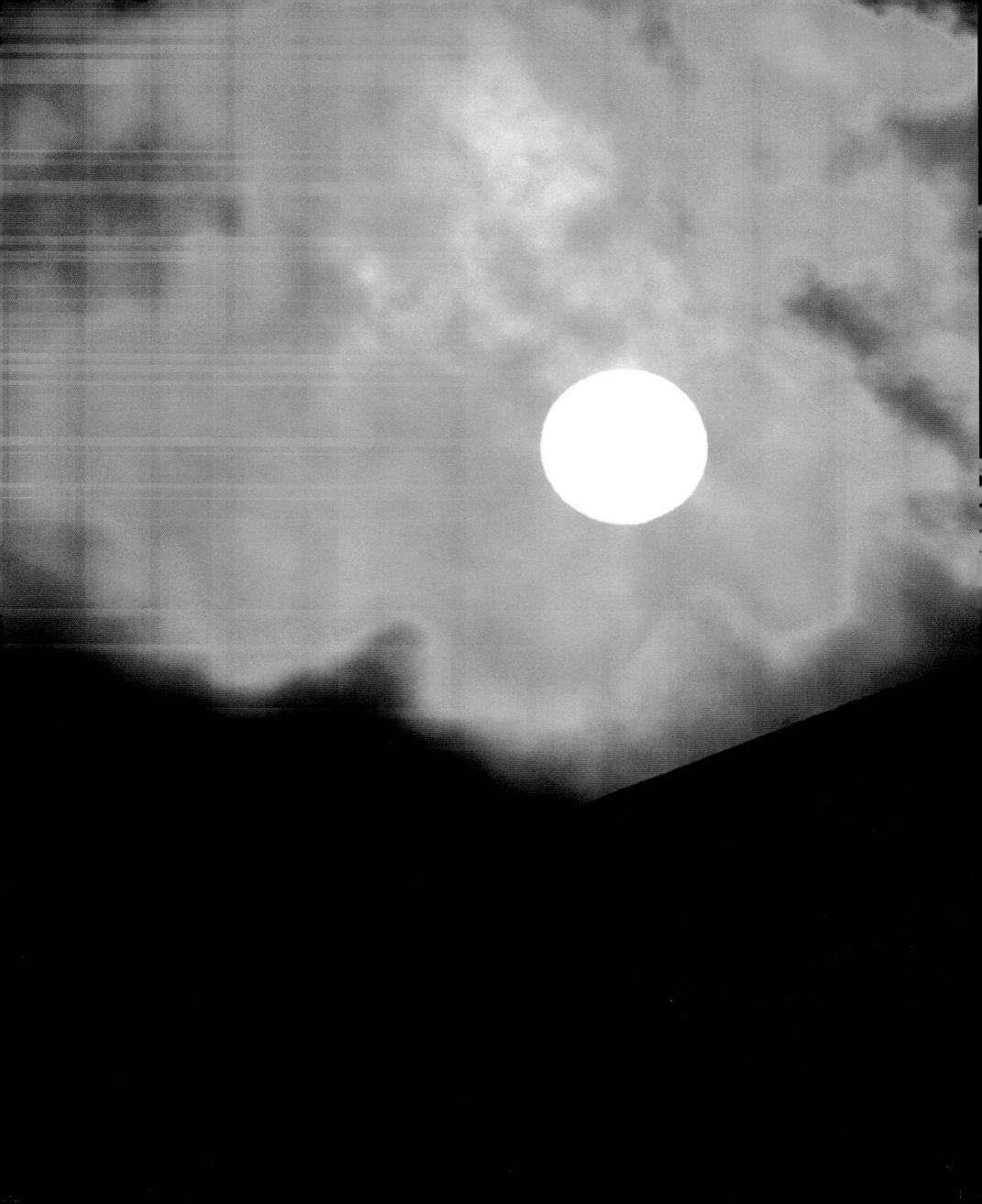

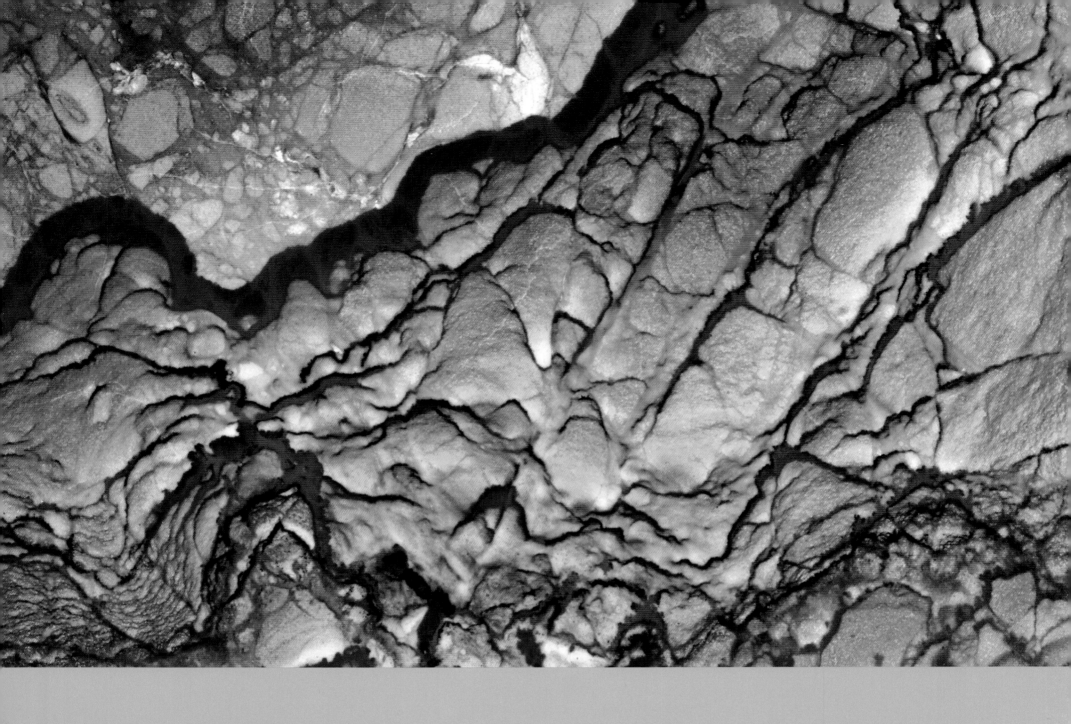

TOP LEFT: Sandstone, South Africa
LEFT: Rhyolite, Utah
ABOVE: Jasper, Oregon
PREVIOUS PAGES:
PAGE 28: Lava River, Hawaii
PAGE 30: Sandstone, Utah
PAGE 31: Cooling Lava, Hawaii
PAGES 32–33: Sun and Volcanic Fumes, Hawaii
PAGE 35: Jasper, Oregon

Every step is a struggle as I follow a team of geologists across a lifeless landscape of fractured black lava. Ahead of us looms the smoking cone of Pu'u 'O'o, the active vent of Kilauea volcano on the Big Island of Hawaii. We follow a torturous route up the flanks, but when we finally reach the rim the reward is a scene from a primordial planet. A roiling lake of liquid lava fills the inside of the crater. Craggy vents belch fountains of red-hot molten rock from deep inside the Earth. When the wind shifts, a blast of heat hits my face and harsh fumes choke my lungs. The air is full of sulfur. This is the smell of early Earth.

Volcanoes dotted the Earth not long after it formed 4.56 billion years ago and its surface solidified. Ever since, volcanoes have been the vents through which Earth has released material from its fiery interior: lava, the liquid substance of the Earth, and gases, the ingredients of the atmosphere. These planetary exhalations of carbon dioxide, nitrogen, water vapor, and other gases formed an early atmosphere—but one that would have been deadly to us because it contained only a trace of oxygen.

I wear a respirator to filter the noxious fumes coming out of Pu'u 'O'o, and even so, it's not a healthy place to stay for long. In the evening we retreat to a spot lower down on the flanks and roll out our sleeping bags on the naked rock. But I do not sleep. After dark Pu'u 'O'o becomes a glowing light show accompanied by a cacophony of earth sounds. It booms and rumbles, it spatters and spits, punctuated by intermittent thundering explosions. Down below us, from a new crack in the Earth, lava flows in incandescent streams. I lie awake in the dark, absorbed in a world reduced to its elements.

LEFT: Volcano Erupting, Hawaii
FOLLOWING PAGES:

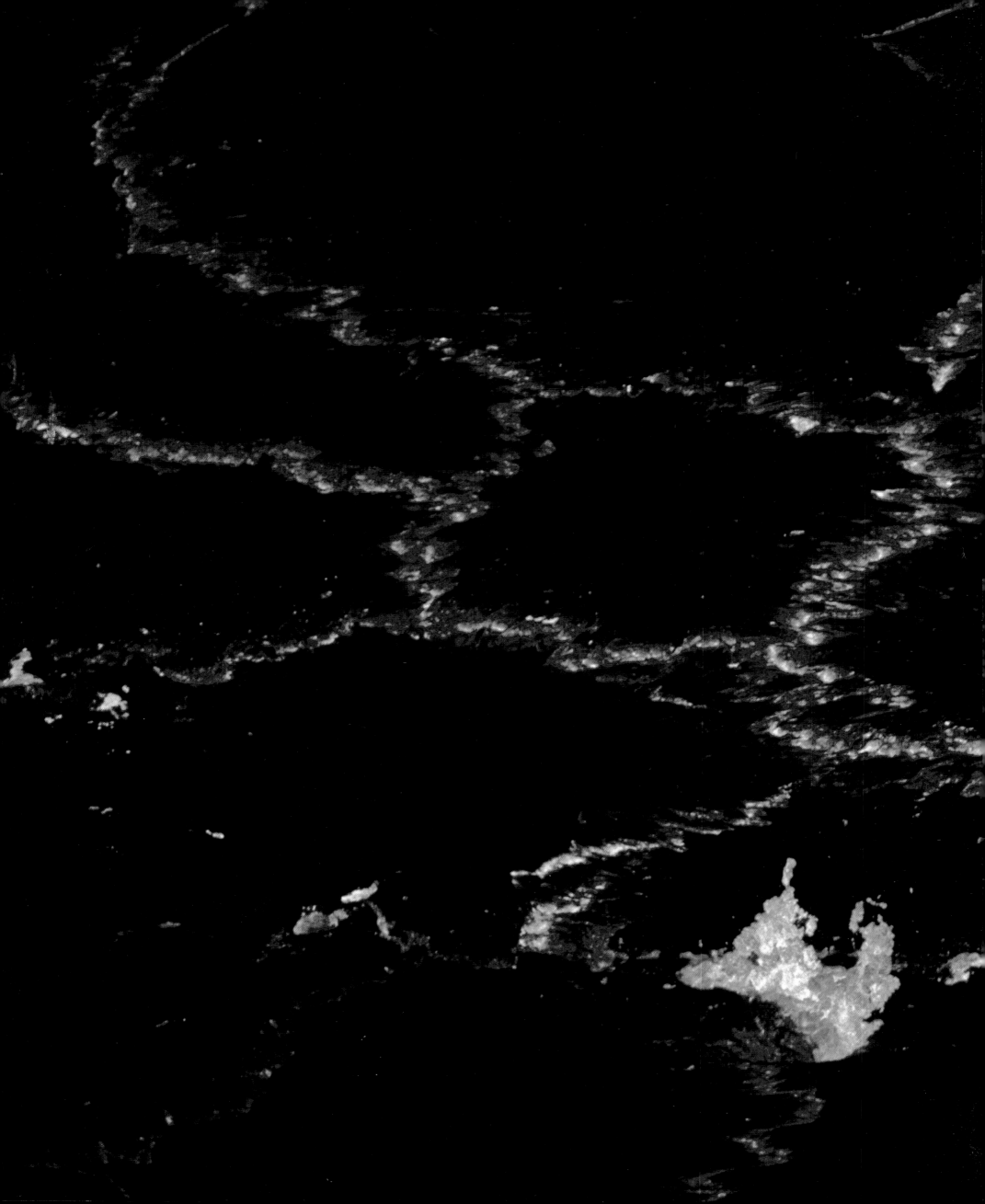

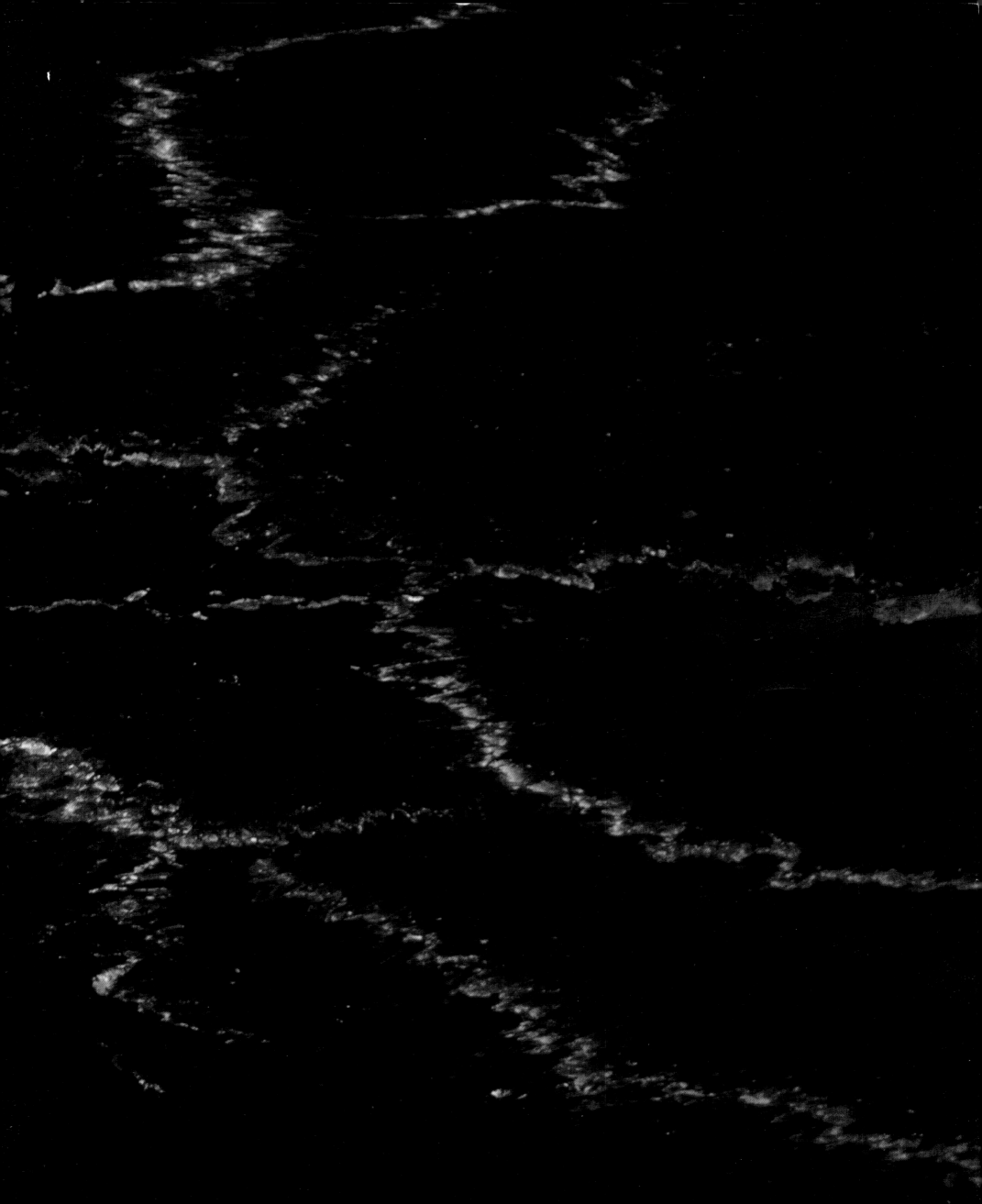

LEFT: Salt Streaks on Mud Flats, Botswana
ABOVE: Moon over Salt Desert, Botswana
FOLLOWING PAGES:
PAGES 52–53: Erosion Patterns, Utah
PAGES 54–55: Icescape, Antarctica

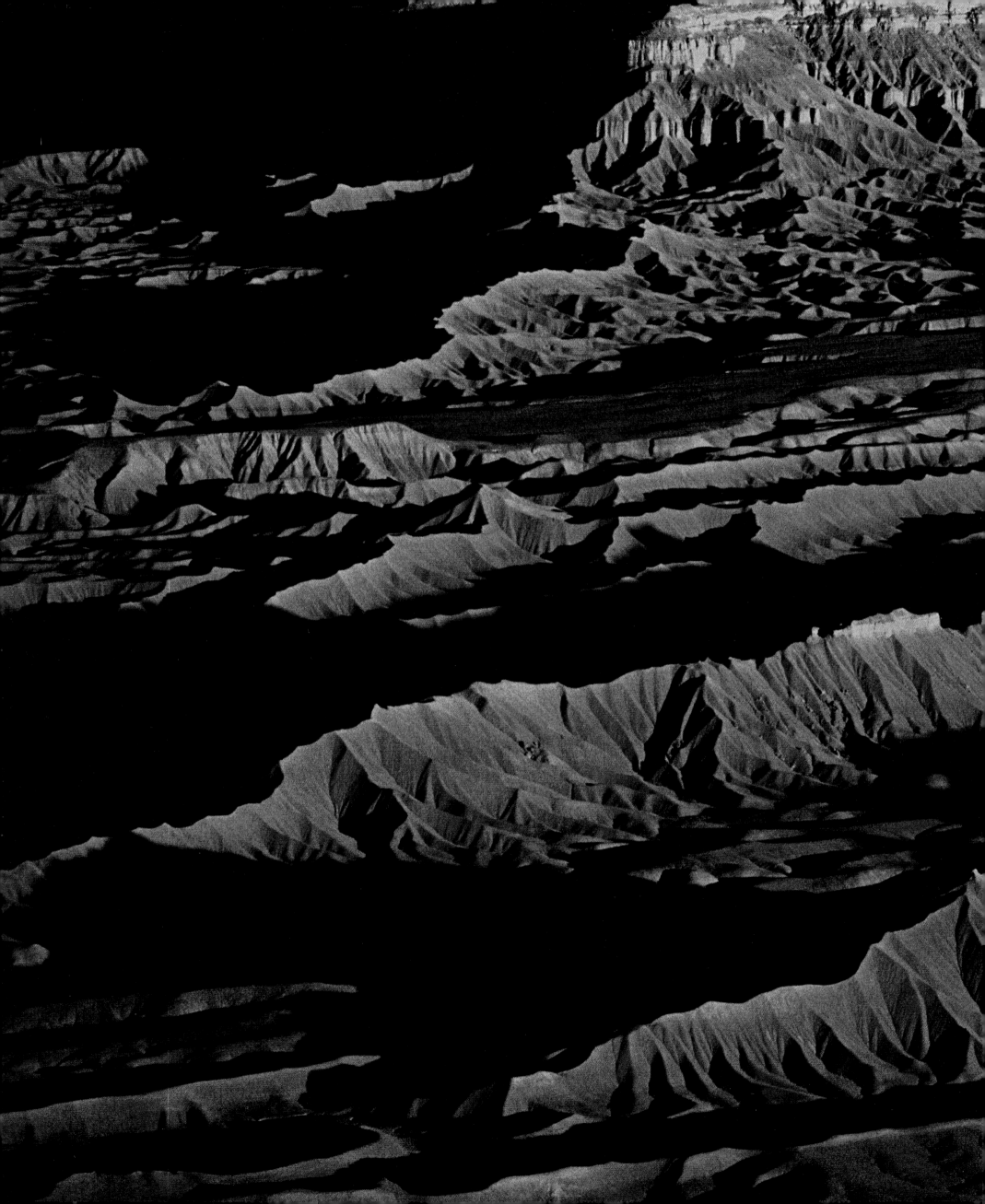

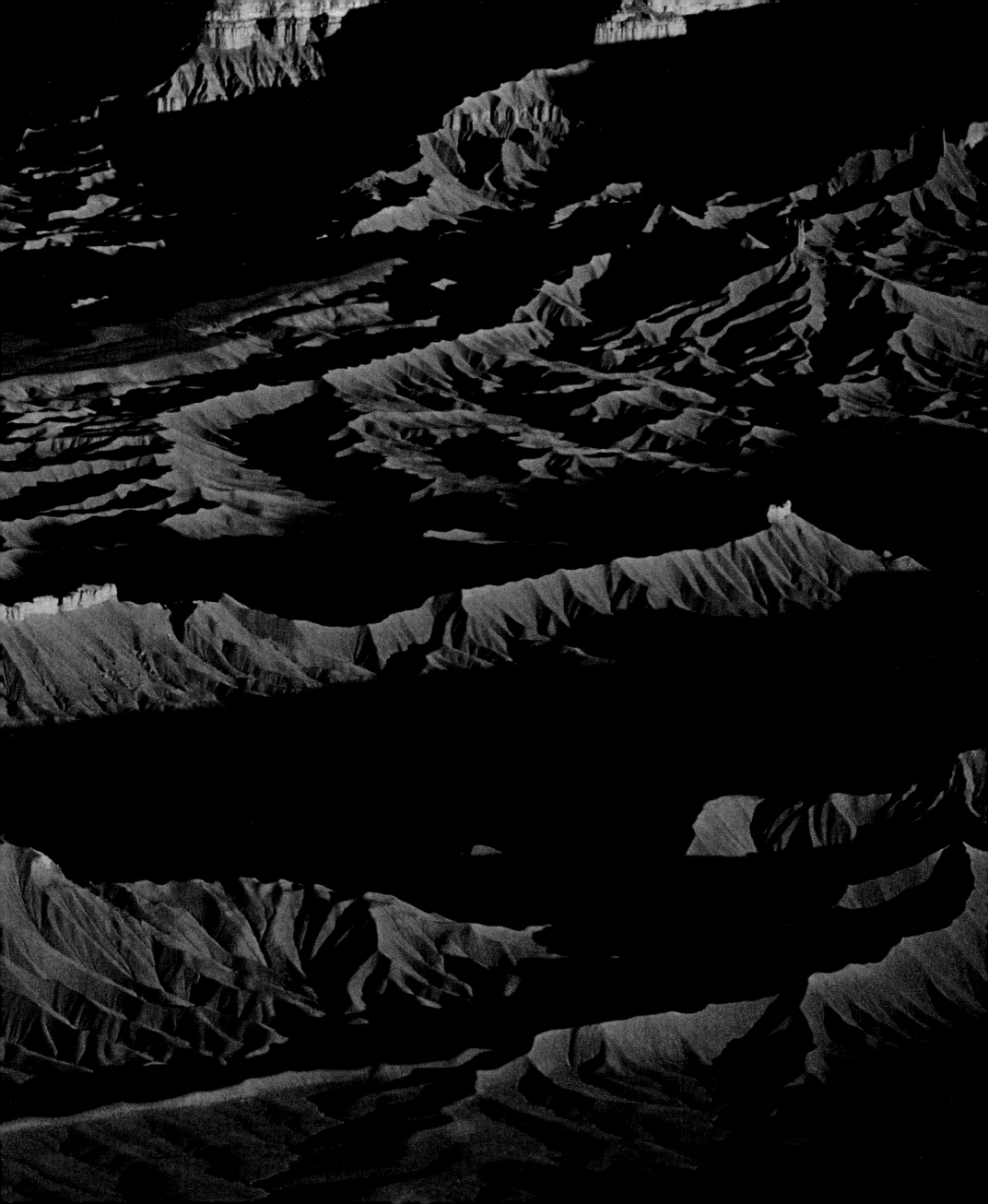

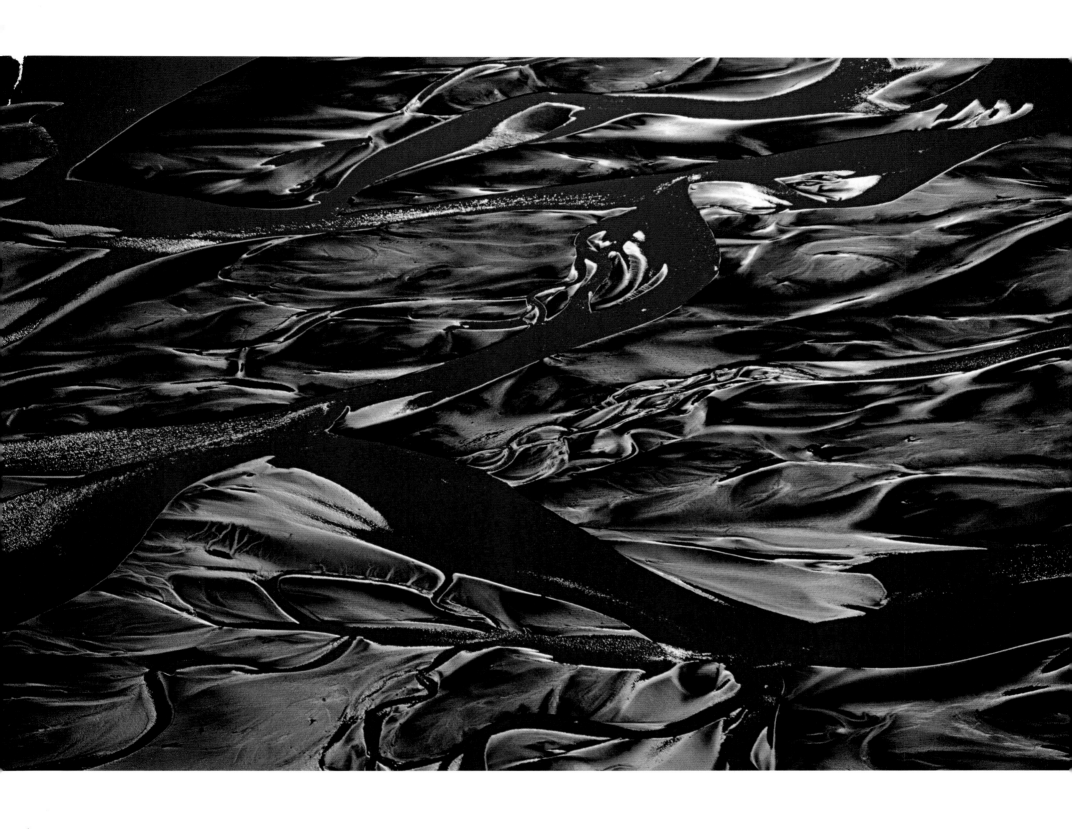

LEFT: Icicles and Sun, Antarctica
ABOVE: Water and Mud Flats, Alaska
FOLLOWING PAGES:
PAGES 58–59: Glacier and Mountains, Alaska

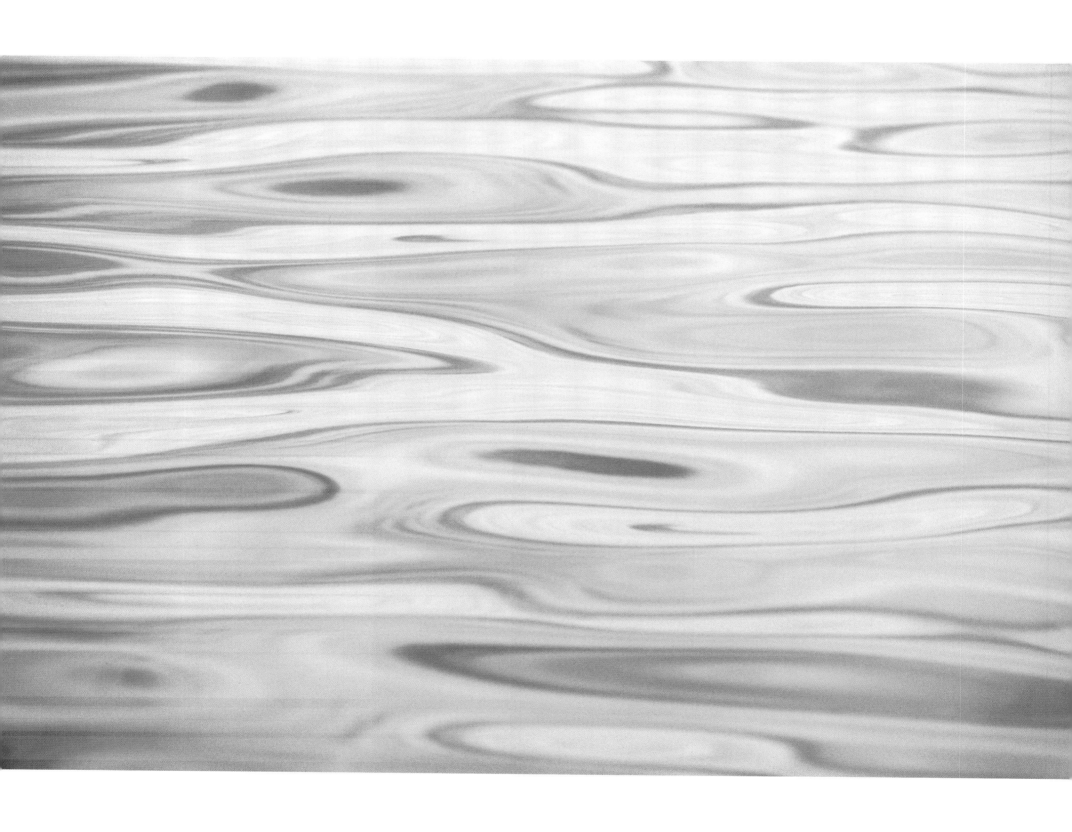

LEFT: Water Reflections, Netherlands
ABOVE: Boiling Mud, New Zealand

BEGINNINGS

In the faint glow of twilight I can just make out their rounded shapes in the water. They look like boulders on the tide line of a rocky beach, but they are alive. They are stromatolites, living reefs built layer by layer by single-celled organisms known as cyanobacteria. As early as three billion years ago the ancestors of these microorganisms began to change the atmosphere, and over time they altered the course of life on Earth. I've come to Shark Bay, a remote lagoon in Western Australia, to see the survivors of this ancient lineage.

The earliest cyanobacteria may have appeared within a few hundred million years after conditions on Earth had become favorable to life. The Earth had cooled, and as water vapor condensed from its atmosphere, torrential rains fell for millions of years and formed the first oceans. When and where life itself first evolved is still unclear, but by the time the cyanobacteria that create stromatolites emerged, the atmosphere was still made up of gases vented by volcanoes. There was virtually no oxygen. The sky was not yet blue.

Cyanobacteria changed that. They were the first life-forms to convert sunlight and water into energy through photosynthesis, releasing oxygen as a by-product. For two billion years—nearly half of Earth's history—massive blooms of cyanobacteria floated in the oceans and stromatolites lined the shores of shallow seas around the world. Collectively cyanobacteria produced so much oxygen that they changed the composition of the atmosphere, and that paved the way for the evolution of all animals afterwards, which depend on oxygen to breathe. Their exhalations also created Earth's ozone layer, which is made of oxygen and shields complex life from deadly ultraviolet radiation. And when oxygen reacted with bacteria-generated methane in the air, organic haze disappeared. As a result, sunlight scatters differently, and the sky now appears blue.

Today stromatolites occur in only a few extreme environments where snails and other marine grazers that feed on cyanobacteria can't survive. A hypersaline lagoon deep inside Shark Bay is such a place. It's a sunny morning and the sky is bright blue when I wade into the water and dive down wearing a face mask for a closer view of the stromatolites. Underwater they look like giant mushrooms anchored in sand. I swim up to one and touch it; its surface is slimy. Minuscule bubbles of oxygen rise from it. I stay underwater as long as I can, but my lungs have a limit: I have to come up for air.

LEFT: Fossil Stromatolites, Bolivia
ABOVE: Banded Iron, Australia
FOLLOWING PAGES:
PAGES 76–77: Diatoms, Harvard University

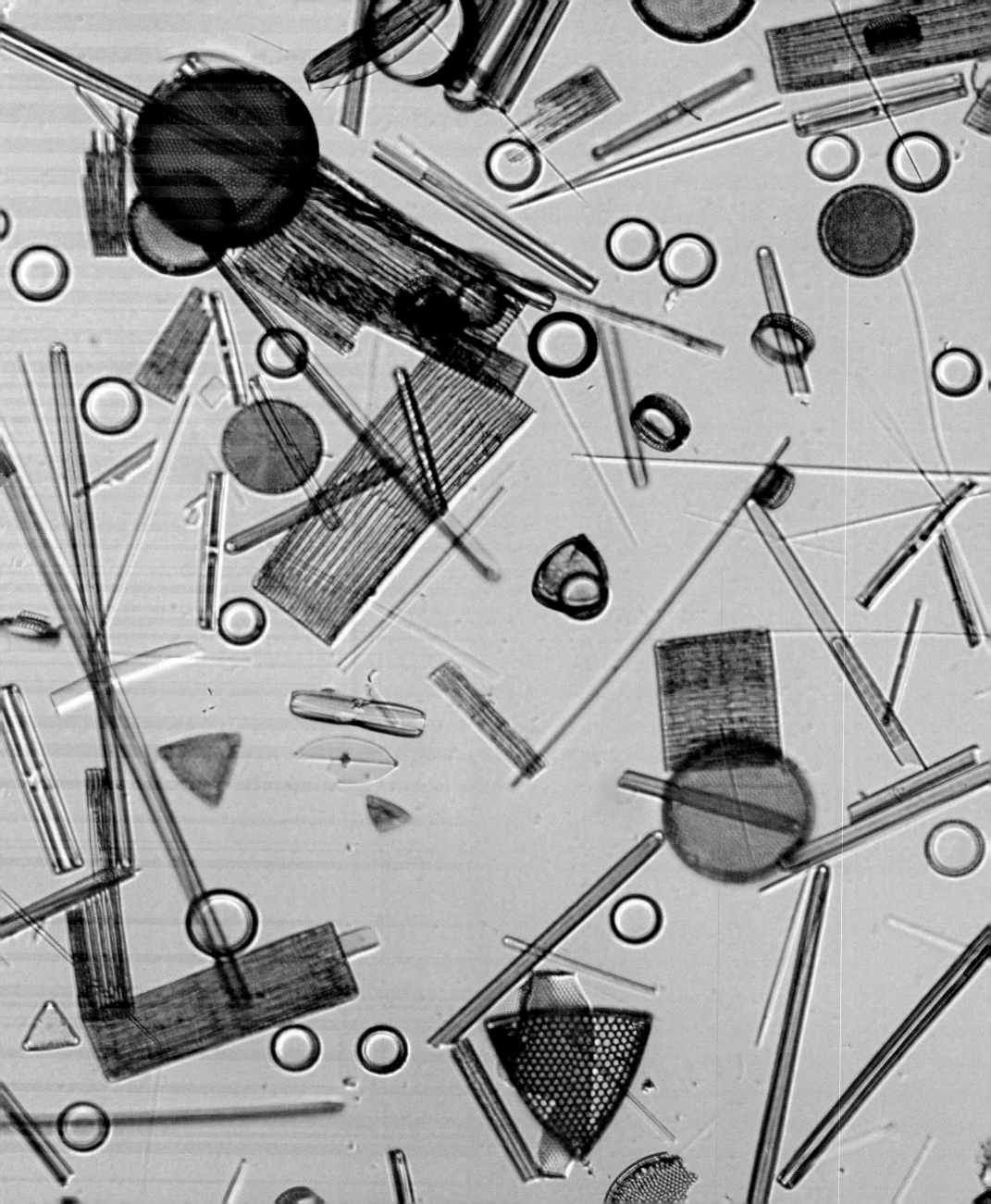

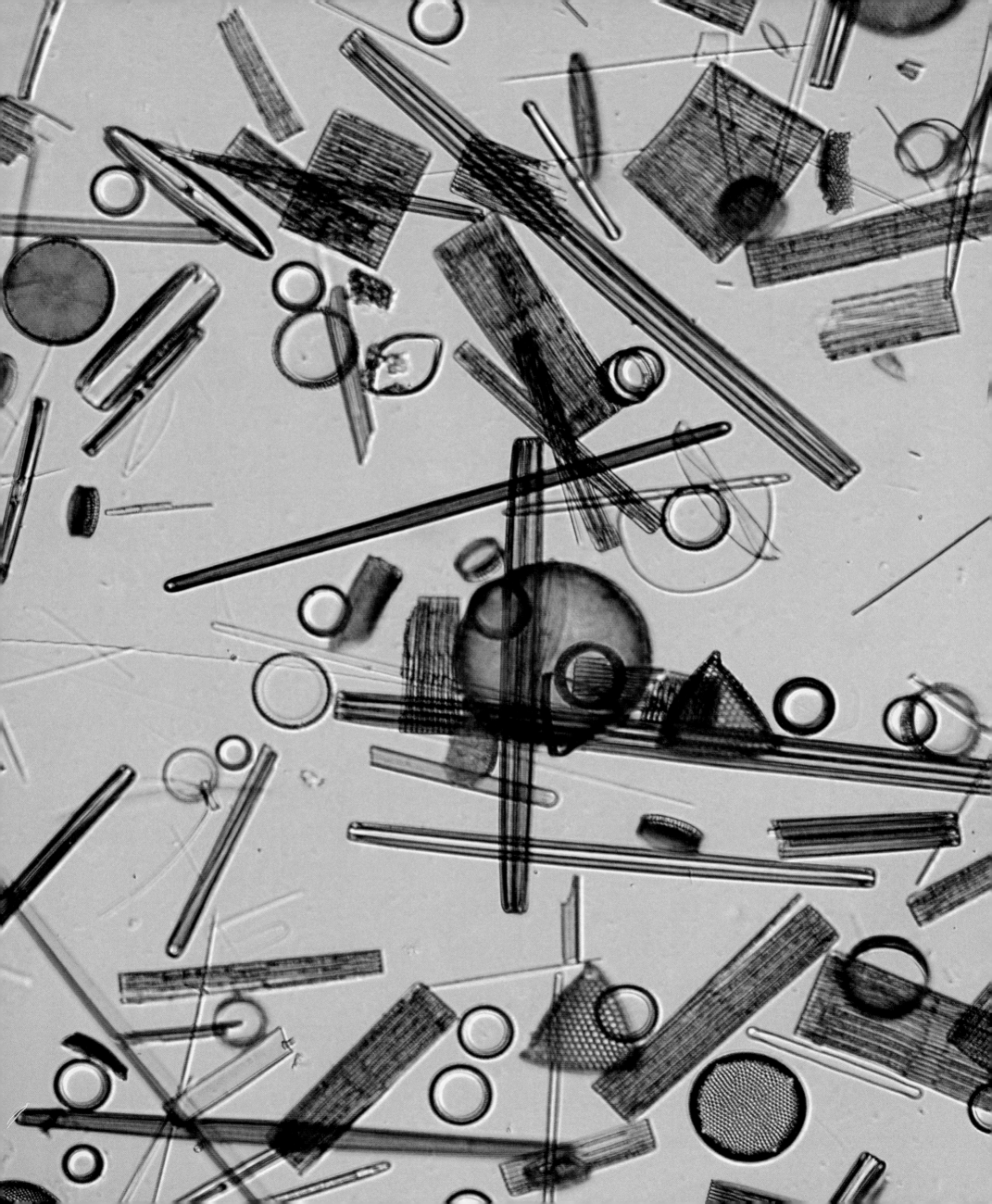

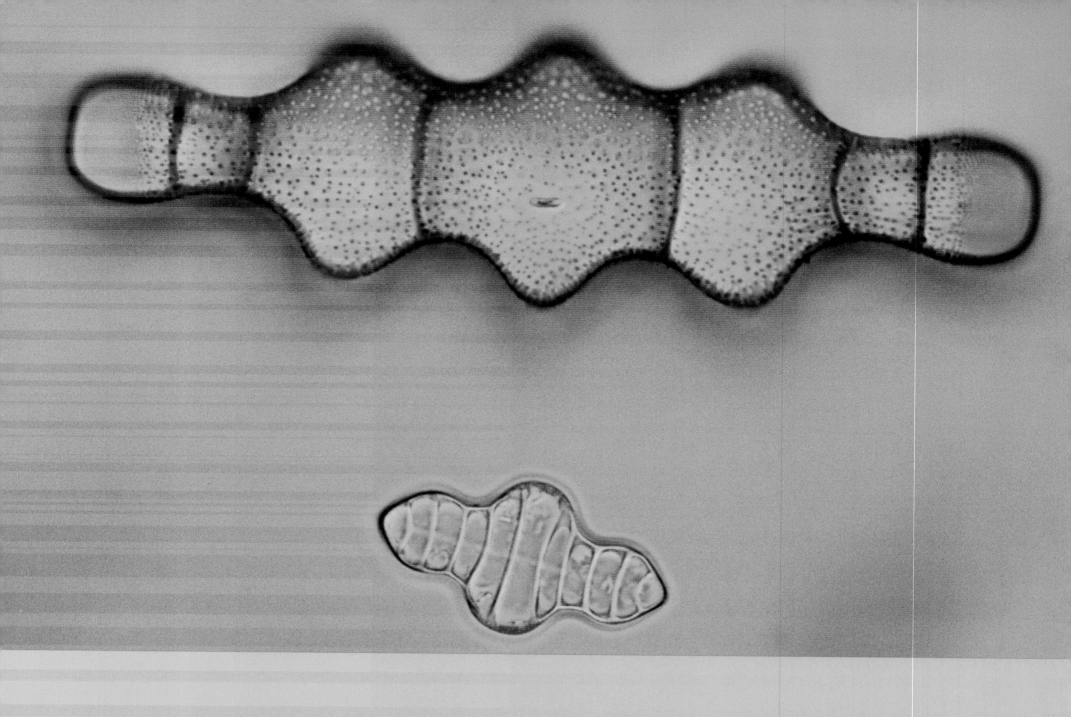

ABOVE: Diatoms, Harvard University
TOP RIGHT AND RIGHT: Diatom, Harvard University
FOLLOWING PAGES:
PAGES 80–81: Diatom, Harvard University

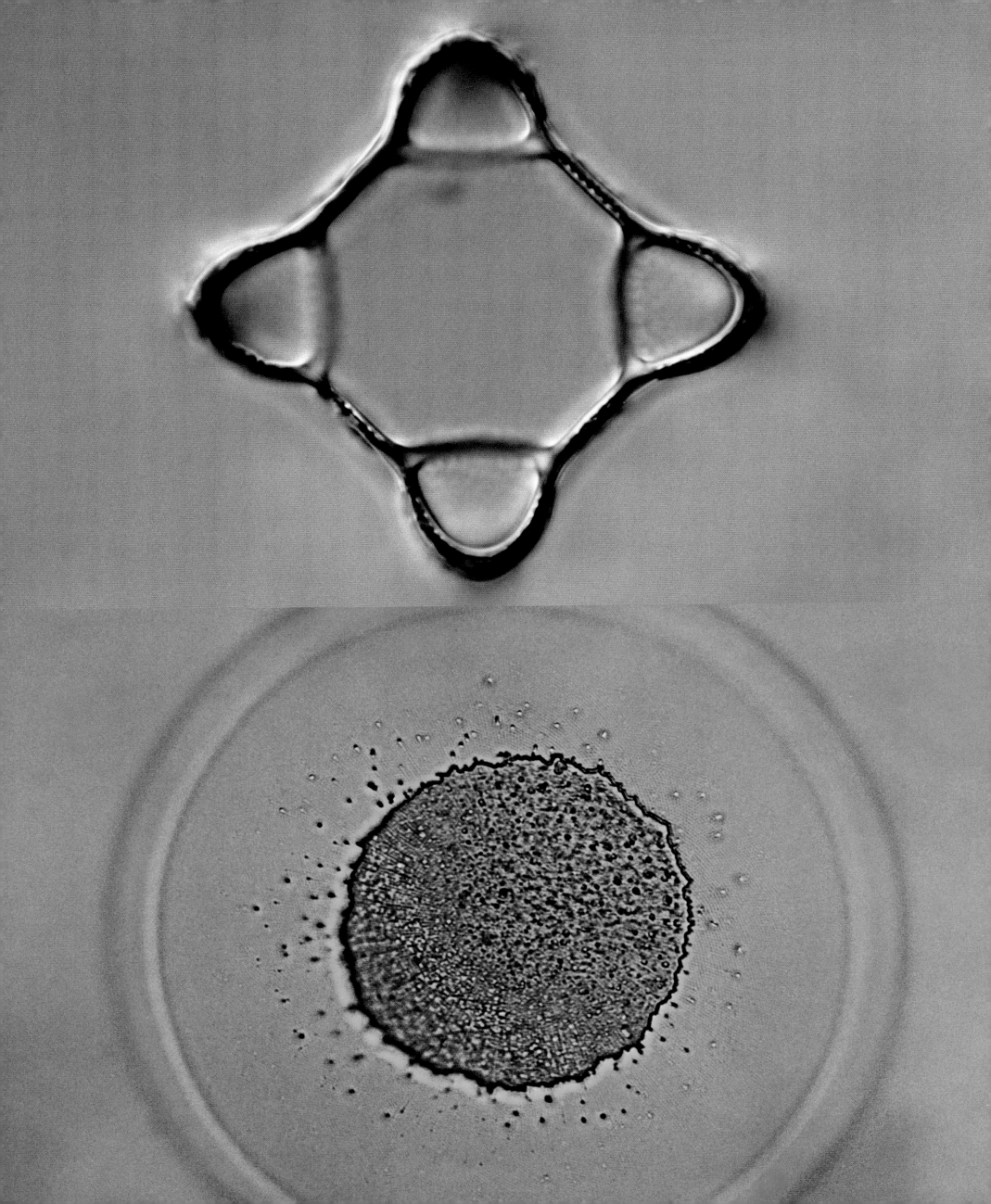

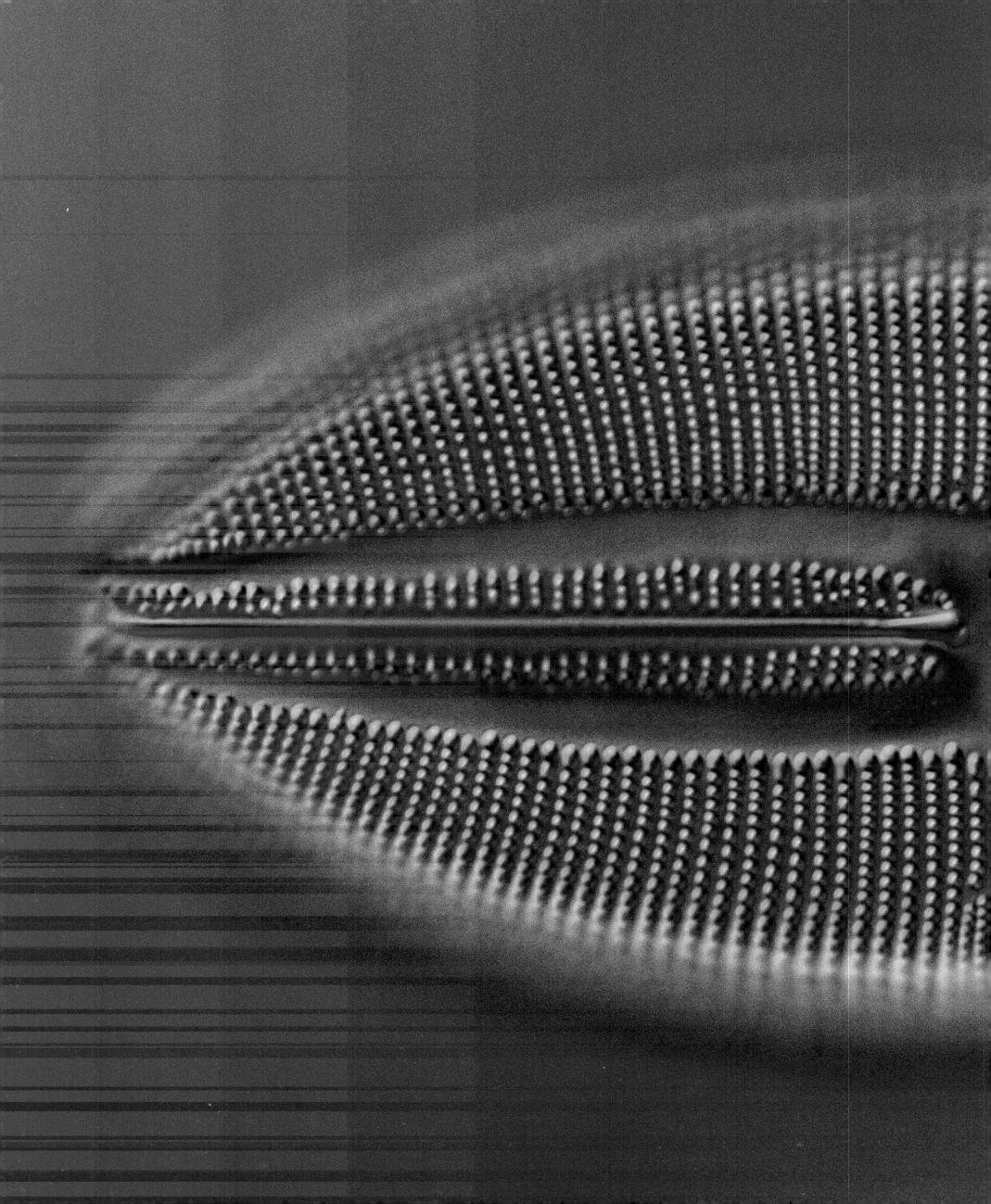

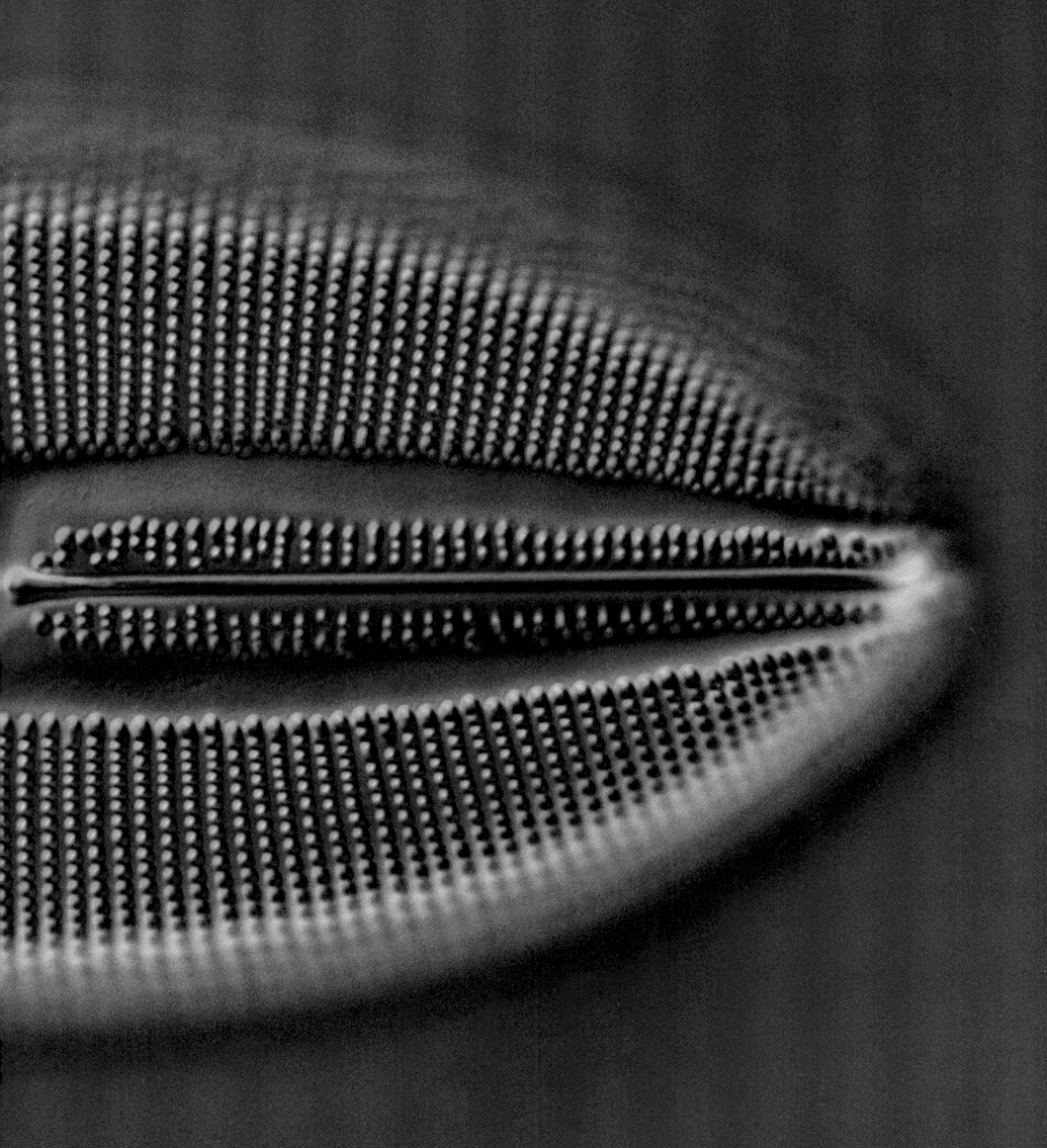

LEFT: Fossil Sea Lilies, Germany
ABOVE: Flower Hat Jelly, California
FOLLOWING PAGES:
PAGE 84: Crystal Jelly, California
PAGE 85: Comb Jelly, California
PAGE 86: Fossil Ammonoid, Germany
PAGE 87: Nautilus Shell, South Pacific Ocean

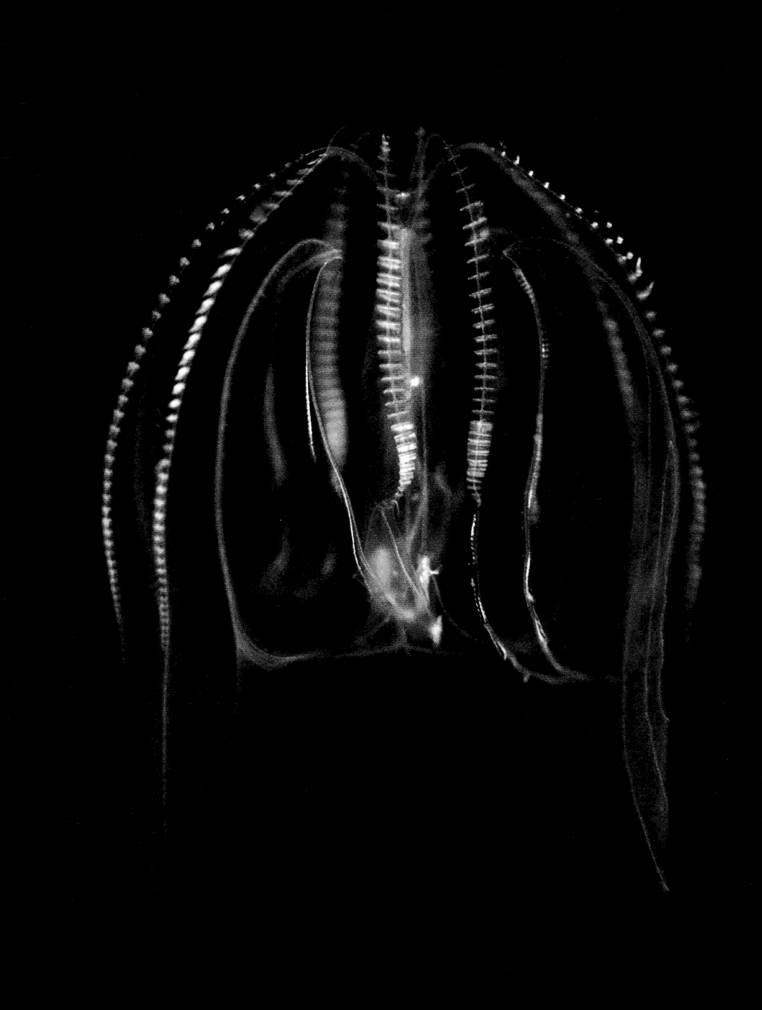

ABOVE: Fossil Trilobite, Canada
RIGHT: Fossil Coral, Indonesia

ABOVE: Coral Polyps, Australia
TOP RIGHT: Staghorn Coral, Australia
RIGHT: Sea Cucumber, Australia
FOLLOWING PAGES:
PAGES 92–93: Schooling Fish, Australia

OUT OF THE SEA

EMERGING

On a calm spring afternoon I went to a beach in Delaware Bay to watch an ancient ritual. As the sun went down and the tide came in, strange creatures began to appear. I could see their helmeted shells break the surface of the water. They were horseshoe crabs, and by twilight thousands were scrambling over each other along the tide line in a scene of primeval fecundity.

Horseshoe crabs are enduring pioneers. For hundreds of millions of years they have inhabited coastal seas from which they emerge each spring to spawn on sheltered beaches when the tide is high and the moon is full.

The seas had gotten crowded 500 million years ago, after a spurt of evolutionary experimentation known as the Cambrian Explosion. There had been a proliferation of new life-forms. The evolution of predators and prey had yielded animals that could see and had shaped creatures with shells within which they could hide. The ancestors of horseshoe crabs arose as predators who pursued worms on the seafloor, but their shells protected them from others who preyed on them.

Even though they were marine in nature, horseshoe crabs developed adaptations for coping out of the water on the seashore. They could handle changes in temperature and salinity, and their shells helped against drying out. That enabled them to adopt a new lifestyle: They began to come out of the sea to spawn and exploit niches on land at a time when it was almost unoccupied around 400 million years ago.

Remarkably, this spawning strategy has survived the odds of time. When horseshoe crabs evolved their habits, there were no other animals on land yet to hinder them. That has changed. When I returned to the beach the next morning the crabs had retreated back into the sea, but thousands of shorebirds were probing the sand to feed on crab eggs, which are pure protein. Life on land has become as crowded as the seas once were.

LEFT: Horseshoe Crabs, Delaware Bay
PREVIOUS PAGES:
PAGE 94: Sea Turtle Tracks, Surinam
PAGE 96: Fossil Eurypterids, New York
PAGE 97: Sally Lightfoot Crabs, Galápagos Islands
FOLLOWING PAGES:
PAGES 100–101: Horseshoe Crab, Delaware Bay
PAGES 102–103: Sally Lightfoot Crab, Galápagos Islands

99

ABOVE: Scorpion, Botswana
RIGHT: Spider Web, California
FOLLOWING PAGES:
PAGES 106–107: Lichen Landscape, Falkland Islands

104

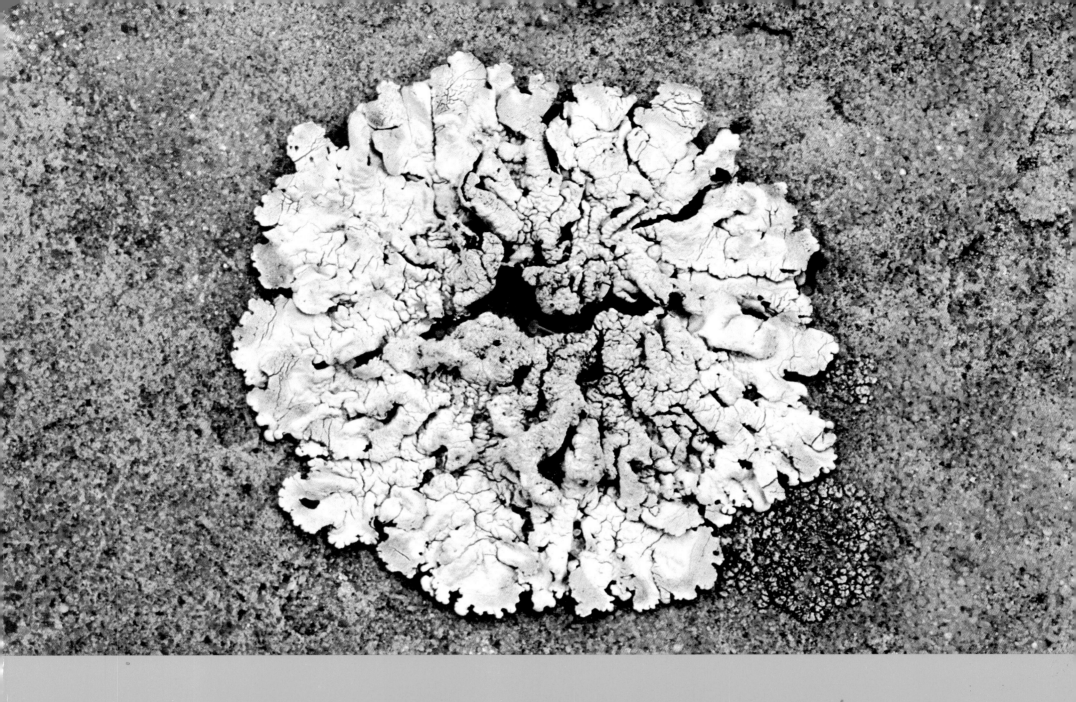

ABOVE: Lichen, Arizona
TOP RIGHT: Lichen Scar, Arizona
RIGHT: Lichen Scars, Arizona
FOLLOWING PAGES:
PAGES 110–111: Whisk Fern, Hawaii
PAGE 112: Unfolding Ferns, Hawaii
PAGE 113: Filmy Fern, New Zealand

ABOVE: Club Moss, Hawaii
TOP RIGHT: Kelp, Falkland Islands
RIGHT: Spike Moss, Florida
FOLLOWING PAGES:
PAGES 116–117: Horsetails, California
PAGE 119: Desert Spadefoot Frog, Australia
PAGE 120: Land Snail, California
PAGE 121: Mudskipper, Australia

RIGHT: Green Sea Turtle Hatchling, Surinam
FOLLOWING PAGES:
PAGES 124–125: Leatherback Sea Turtle, Surinam

ON LAND

Nothing stirs. The tortoises are all asleep. It's night but there's a full moon overhead that illuminates a world that is trapped in time. I've been here for a week at the summit of Alcedo volcano in the Galápagos Islands to observe giant tortoises. They're old-timers who live life slowly. They sleep until mid-morning and move less than a hundred yards in a day to forage on plants that they barely digest. They take long siestas and by five in the afternoon they're asleep again for the night.

The tortoise way of life is typical for cold-blooded reptiles, whose great diversification into dinosaurs, pterosaurs, crocodiles, and many other forms began around 230 million years ago. Back then conditions on Earth were predominantly warm and dry, and that stimulated the evolution of reptiles on land. Their bodies were protected with waterproof, scaly skin and their metabolism minimized the need for drinking water. And, in a breakthrough that enabled them to colonize the interiors of continents, they produced eggs with membranes that sealed in fluids and could develop away from water.

Female tortoises of Alcedo undertake a long journey to lay their eggs. They ramble down the slopes of the volcano through treacherous lava flows to reach the warm lowlands. It may take them weeks to arrive at the right spot, where they dig a nest hole with their hind feet, deposit their eggs, and seal it up with sand. They never look back, and leave the incubation of their eggs to the sun. It can take more than four months before the young ones hatch, crawl out of the ground, and have to fend for themselves.

The tortoises of Galápagos provide a glimpse back in time to an era dominated by reptilian giants. But most cold-blooded animals do not easily adapt to changing climates or new opportunities. Some large reptiles, by virtue of their mass, can maintain a body temperature that is not dependent on exterior warmth alone, but smaller reptiles cannot regulate their body temperature internally. When warm-blooded animals evolved they gained an edge, and most cold-blooded reptiles were eventually relegated to narrower niches. Nowadays, large land reptiles like giant tortoises prevail only in a few isolated places like the Galápagos Islands that have no native mammals. But even this time capsule has been pierced. Feral goats introduced by humans are invading Alcedo. They move fast, they multiply fast, and they're eating their way through the tortoises' placid environment. In the dark I can hear them bleating, noisy newcomers to this scene of tranquillity.

LEFT: Giant Tortoises by Moonlight, Galápagos Islands
PREVIOUS PAGES:
PAGES 132–133: Palm Savanna, Madagascar
PAGES 134–135: Tuatara, New Zealand

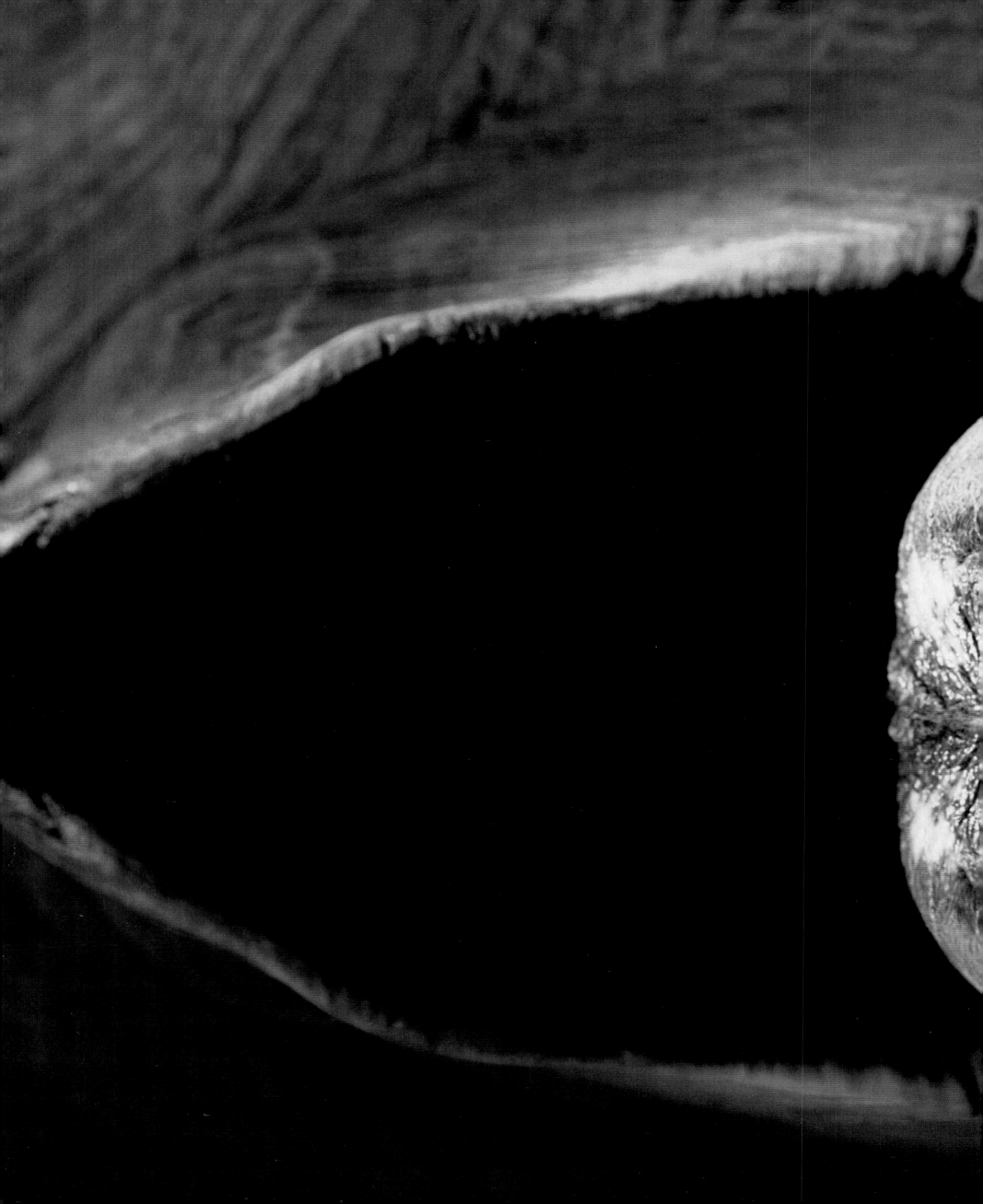

LEFT: Marine Iguanas, Galápagos Islands
ABOVE: Crocodile Hatchling, Botswana
PREVIOUS PAGES:
PAGES 138–139: Giant Tortoise, Galápagos Islands

ABOVE: Jackson's Chameleon, Kenya
TOP RIGHT: Thorny Devil, Australia
RIGHT: Blue-tongued Skink, Australia
FOLLOWING PAGES:
PAGES 144–145: Crocodiles, Botswana
PAGES 146–147: Sand Dunes, Australia
PAGE 149: Tree Fern Forest, New Zealand
PAGES 150–151: Redwoods, California
PAGES 152–153: Spruces in Snow, Finland

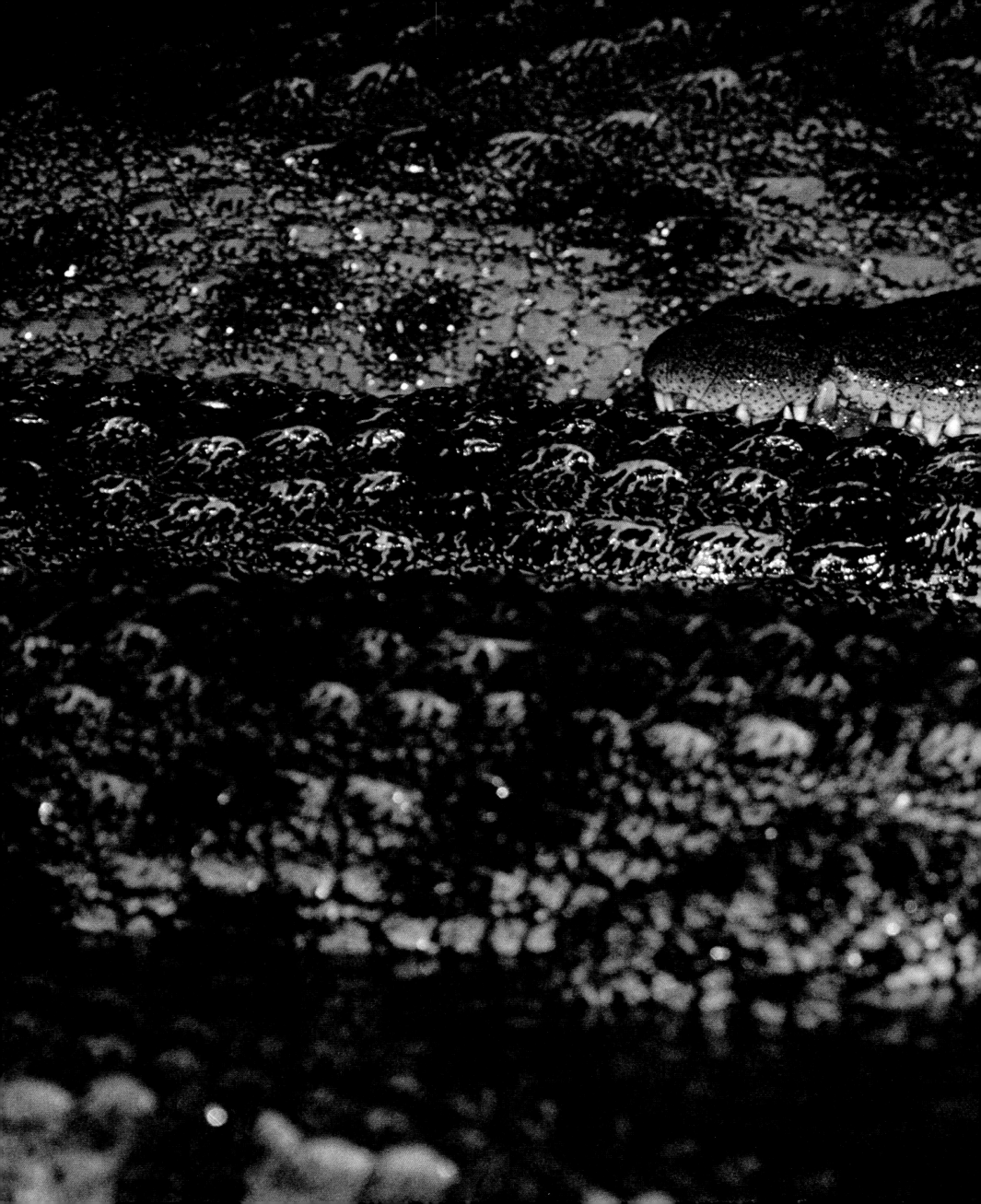

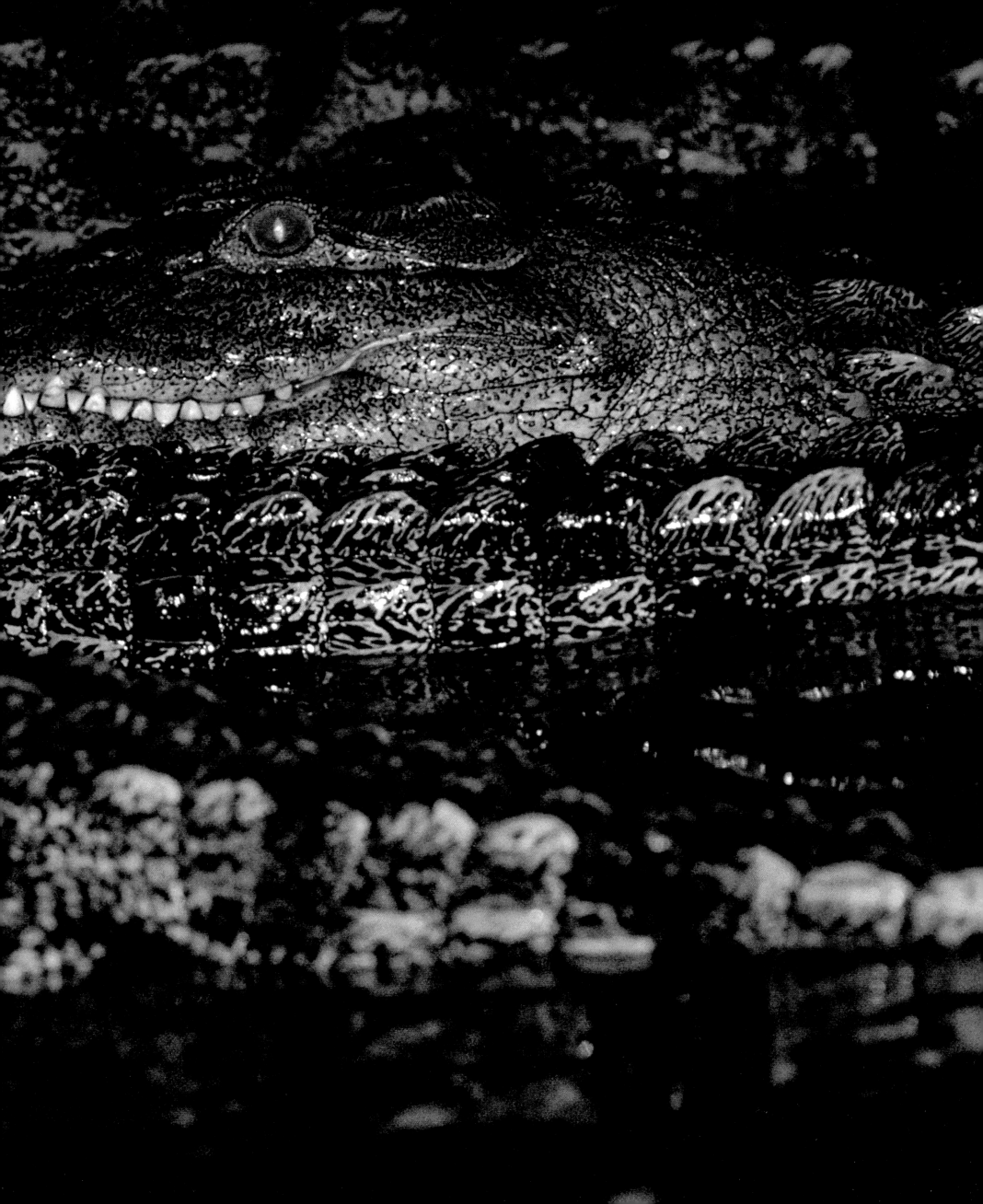

INTO THE AIR

I'm sitting on the beach of a tiny island in the middle of the Pacific Ocean, watching an albatross fly. Without a single flap, it glides effortlessly on outstretched wings, coasting down toward the water to build up speed before it sweeps up into the wind for a steep climb. When the bird almost stalls, 50 feet above the ocean, it banks and starts another downward glide. At first glance it may seem like a roundabout way to fly, but it is actually highly efficient. Like a windsurfer, the albatross utilizes the wind's energy to propel itself. Albatrosses spend most of their lives searching for squid and fish on the open ocean, and they have to be able to travel great distances without expending much energy. One Laysan albatross, like the bird I'm watching here in the Hawaiian Leeward Islands, once covered 3,200 miles in a single ten-day trip.

Albatrosses represent one extreme example of life adapting to the air, but they are not without precedent. Before birds evolved, some reptiles had already become capable of flight. Pterosaurs evolved light skeletons and their forelimbs extended into struts that supported long, narrow wings. One of them, *Quetzalcoatlus*, grew into the largest creature ever to take to the air. With a wingspan of nearly 40 feet, it was the size of a small passenger plane. Scientists believe that some pterosaurs were capable of flapping flight, but many of them must have been soarers or gliders. Most pterosaur fossils have been found near the sea, where they flourished for more than 150 million years. When they went extinct, birds had an opportunity to move into ecological niches left empty by their demise. Some birds became ocean nomads and evolved into albatrosses, but their ingenious use of wind currents near the water surface is only one way to fly.

When I look up into the sky, I can see tiny specks. They are frigatebirds, riding thermals of warm air. Their superlight bodies are geared for soaring. Frigatebirds go up as high as 10,000 feet and use that altitude to cover long distances. They can stay in the air day and night; they fish, and even sleep, on the wing.

By looking at frigatebirds and albatrosses, it is possible to imagine the flight of pterosaurs, even though those flying dragons perished as a result of the asteroid that hit Earth 65 million years ago. That same impact may have killed all large dinosaurs, but we now know that some of the smaller ones survived after all. They were the ones that had developed feathers, and turned into birds.

LEFT: Albatross, Hawaii
PREVIOUS PAGES:
PAGE 154: Flamingos, Botswana
PAGE 156: *Archaeopteryx* Fossil, Germany
PAGE 157: Frigatebird, Galápagos Islands

LEFT: Black Heron, Botswana
ABOVE: Water Lily, Botswana
PREVIOUS PAGES:
PAGES 160–161: Sooty Terns, Hawaii
PAGE 162: Bird of Paradise Feathers, Native to New Guinea
PAGE 163: Gull Feather, California

ABOVE: Protea Flower, South Africa
RIGHT: Ant on *Euphorbia* Flower, South Africa
PREVIOUS PAGES:
PAGE 166: Giant Water Lily, Brazil
PAGE 167: *Pachypodium* Flower, South Africa

LEFT: Sunbird and Protea Flower, South Africa
ABOVE: Hummingbird and Ginger Flower, Costa Rica
FOLLOWING PAGES:
PAGE 172: Kakapo, New Zealand
PAGE 173: Kiwi, New Zealand

LEFT: Silversword, Hawaii
FOLLOWING PAGES:
PAGES 176–177: Octopus Trees, Madagascar

ABOVE: Aloe, Madagascar
RIGHT: King Protea, South Africa
FOLLOWING PAGES:
PAGES 180–181: Palo Santo Trees, Galápagos Islands

LEFT: Baobabs, Madagascar
ABOVE: Grass Trees, Australia
FOLLOWING PAGES:
PAGES 184–185: Buttressed Trees, Belize

183

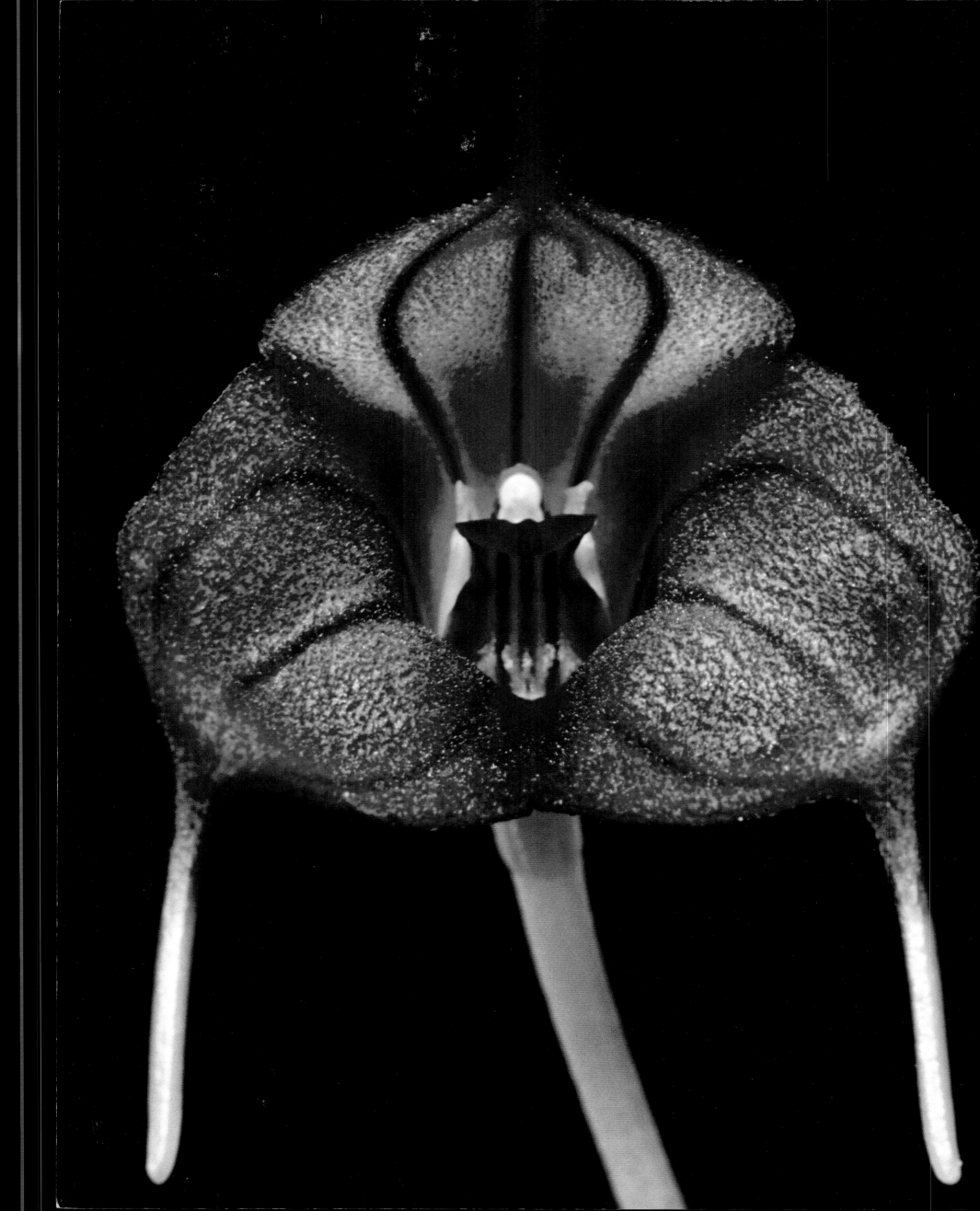

OUT OF THE DARK

LEFT: Flying Fox, Australia
ABOVE: Civet, Borneo
PREVIOUS PAGES:
PAGE 198: Elephant and Kudu, Botswana
PAGE 200: Giant Hedgehog Skull, Italy
PAGE 201: Treeshrew, Borneo

LEFT: Hyena, Botswana
ABOVE: Maned Wolf, Brazil

RIGHT: Giant Anteater, Brazil
FOLLOWING PAGES:
PAGES 208–209: Sea Lions, California

ABOVE: Spinner Dolphin, Hawaii
RIGHT: Beluga, Canada

LEFT: Kangaroo, Australia
ABOVE: Takhi, Mongolia
FOLLOWING PAGES:
PAGES 214–215: Zebras, Kenya
PAGES 216–217: Impalas, Botswana

LEFT: Cheetah, Namibia
ABOVE: Impala, Kenya

A bull elephant has come to drink less than 30 feet from where I am lying flat on the ground at the edge of an African waterhole. He is so close that I can feel his low rumblings vibrating through the ground. He is big and I am vulnerable, but I gamble on his acceptance of me by staying still and passive.

Elephants are the last surviving members of an ancient order of trunked giants, the Proboscidea, which began to proliferate around 50 million years ago and evolved into more than a hundred species, including true elephants as well as mastodons and mammoths, their close relatives. They adapted to virtually every terrestrial environment on Earth, from swamps to savannas, from forests to deserts, and even to the Arctic. They crisscrossed Africa, they wandered in and out of Europe and Asia, and they spread throughout the Americas.

Elephants are symbols of the Pleistocene, an era that lasted from 1.8 million years ago until 10,000 years ago, when the last Ice Age ended. Gigantic mammals of many kinds populated the Pleistocene Earth. During most of this period elephants and their relatives were more widespread than humans, but that changed when our ancestors moved out of Africa and into other continents, around 70,000 years ago. In Europe and Asia hunting cultures developed in which elephants became important resources. But in some places, not long after humans moved in, elephants vanished. When the Americas were colonized by humans from Asia, perhaps around 15,000 years ago, mammoths and mastodons thrived from Alaska to Patagonia. Within a few thousand years, they were gone. Was it due to climate change? Or was it us? According to one theory, human hunters rapidly wiped out an innocent megafauna that had no effective defense because they had never seen humans before.

Ironically, the largest numbers of elephants occur today where they have lived together with us the longest. In Africa elephants were witnesses to our evolution. They saw hominids become humans who turned into skillful hunters. Is it their long coexistence with us that has enabled elephants to survive in Africa, as some suggest? I am not sure if that is the only reason, but I do know that elephants are astute at reading human intentions.

The Pleistocene is very much alive in front of me. The big bull rumbles and flares his ears. He raises himself to express his dominance. He shakes his head and blows a trunkful of dust my way. Then he turns and walks away: He has made his point. At least here, for now, there seems to be enough room for both of us.

LEFT: Elephant and Impala, Botswana
FOLLOWING PAGES:
PAGES 222–223: Elephants, Impalas, and Doves, Botswana
PAGES 224–225: Rainforest, Borneo

ABOVE: Tarsier, Borneo
RIGHT: Sifaka, Madagascar

226

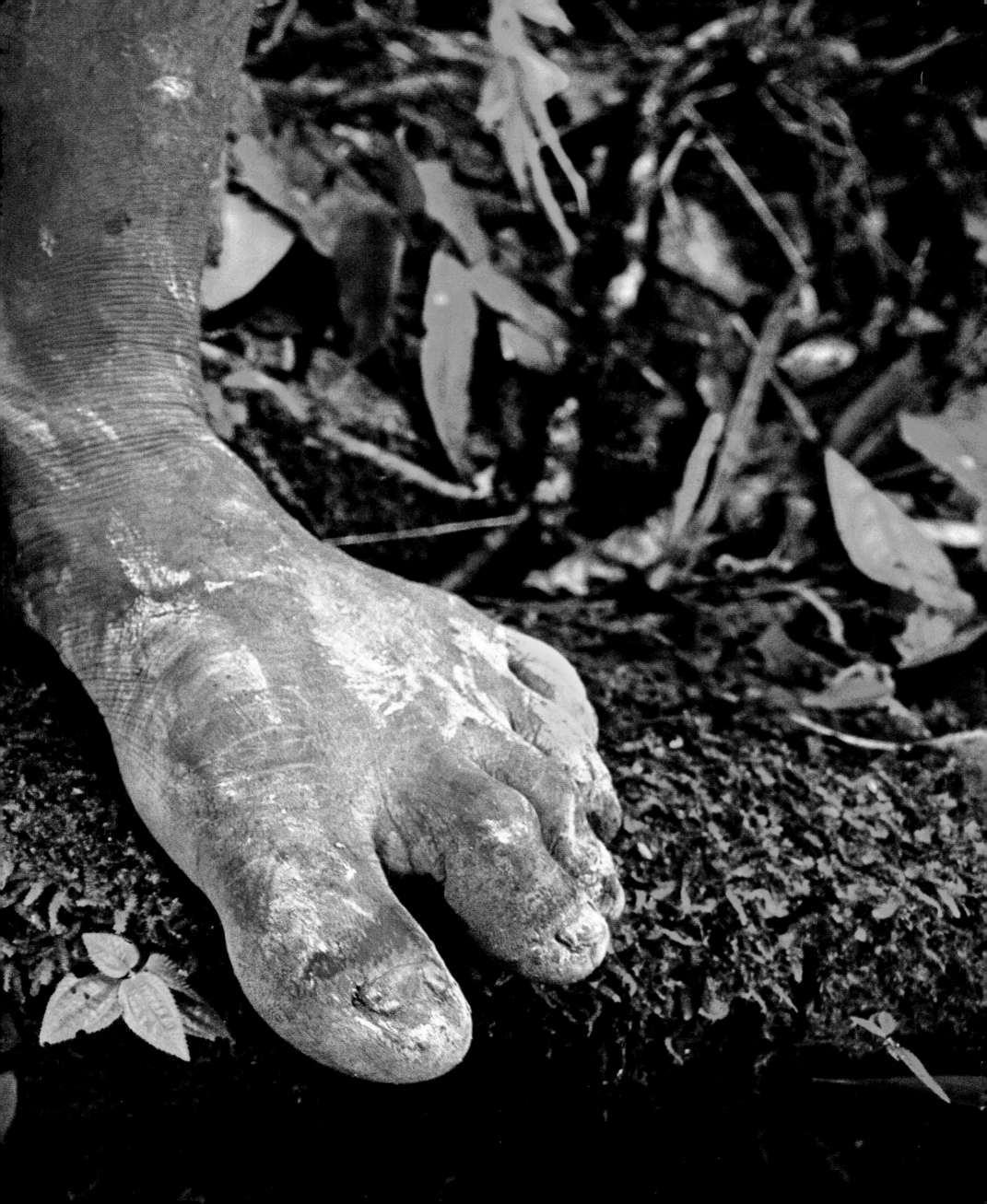

RIGHT: Human Fetus
PREVIOUS PAGES:
PAGE 229: Bonobo and Infant, Native to the Congo Basin
PAGE 230: Chimpanzee, Kenya
PAGE 231: Bonobo, Native to the Congo Basin
PAGES 232–233: Human Feet, Peru
FOLLOWING PAGES:
PAGE 236: Blood Veins in Human Hand
PAGE 237: Braiding River, Alaska

PLANET OF LIFE

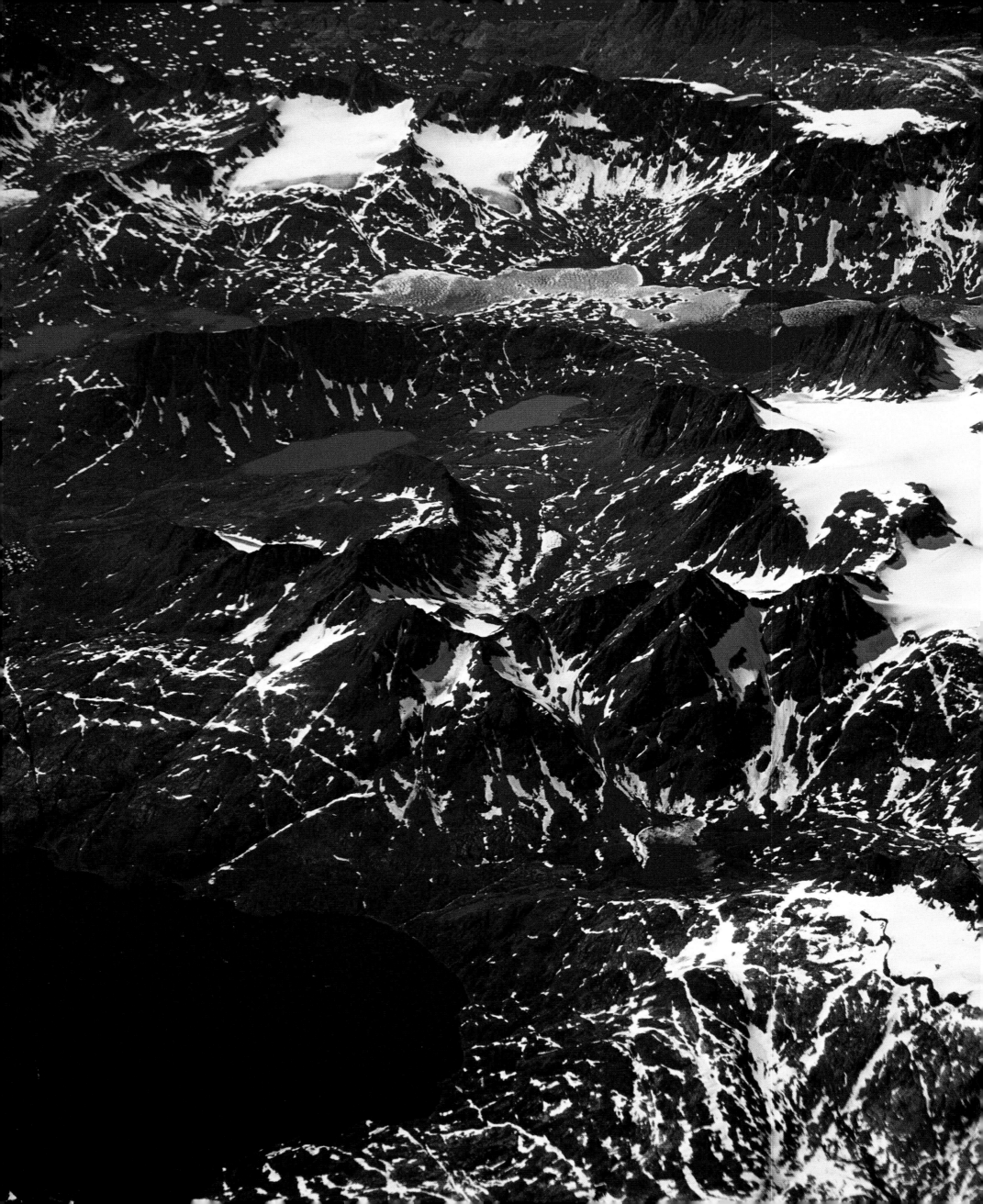

Less than two inches of man-made materials separate me from the thin air seven miles above the Earth. Yet I am comfortable, reclining in a window seat on a jetliner cruising over Greenland at 35,000 feet on a flight from the Netherlands, where I grew up, to California, where I live now. Outside the temperature is minus 58 degrees Fahrenheit, yet even here, life exists. Many microscopic organisms and spores of fungi and ferns have been found at this altitude. After four billion years of evolution, life has spread nearly everywhere on Earth. And it has become a force in its own right.

The idea that life as a whole can be regarded as an entity that interacts with the Earth was postulated by scientist James Lovelock in the 1970s. After comparing Earth's atmosphere with those of other planets in our solar system, Lovelock realized that its composition, with one-fifth oxygen, was highly unusual, yet appeared to be stable over time. He concluded, in a flash of imagination, that Earth's atmosphere should be considered a nonliving extension of life itself. He theorized that the combined biochemical activity of all living organisms was essential to maintaining an atmosphere that keeps Earth hospitable to life. Lovelock named his hypothesis Gaia, after the Greek goddess of the Earth. His provocative ideas were initially rejected by most scientists, but they have since gained in acceptance. Whether life actually regulates conditions on Earth has become part of an ongoing debate, but that it influences them is no longer in dispute.

When the plane approaches California, my attention shifts from a global view of life to an appreciation of where I live. As we descend to San Francisco I can see the coast stretch away to Monterey Bay, my home for more than two decades. I settled here because of its natural beauty. But now, at the end of my journey through time, I view this landscape differently. The textured chronicle of its history has turned me into a time traveler even when I am home. The plants in the coastal meadow that surrounds my house make me think of a time when mammoths and giant ground sloths were part of this ecosystem. The towering redwoods I see from my living room remind me of an ancient age when dinosaurs roamed here. And hiding among the grasses are subtle echoes of even earlier eras: spiders and snails, humble pioneers of life's experimentation with an existence on land. I recognize them now, as I do myself, as separate strands of life, woven together by time into a tapestry of nature that is connected in the present as well as linked to the past.

LEFT: Summer over Greenland
PREVIOUS PAGE 238: Rainforest and Mountains, Brazil;
PAGE 240: Volcanic Caldera, New Zealand; PAGE 241: Meandering River, Peru
FOLLOWING PAGES 244–245: Winter over Greenland; PAGES 246–247: Tundra Autumn, Alaska;
PAGES 248–249: Fall Colors, Alaska; PAGES 250–251: Glacial Valley, Alaska; PAGES 252–253: Coastline, California; PAGE 254: Seagrass Meadows, Australia; PAGE 255: Coral Reefs, Australia; PAGES 256–257: Tidal Surge, New Zealand; PAGES 258–259: Waterfalls, Argentina; PAGES 260–261: Morning Mist over Rainforest, Borneo; PAGES 262–263: Monsoon Clouds, Indian Ocean

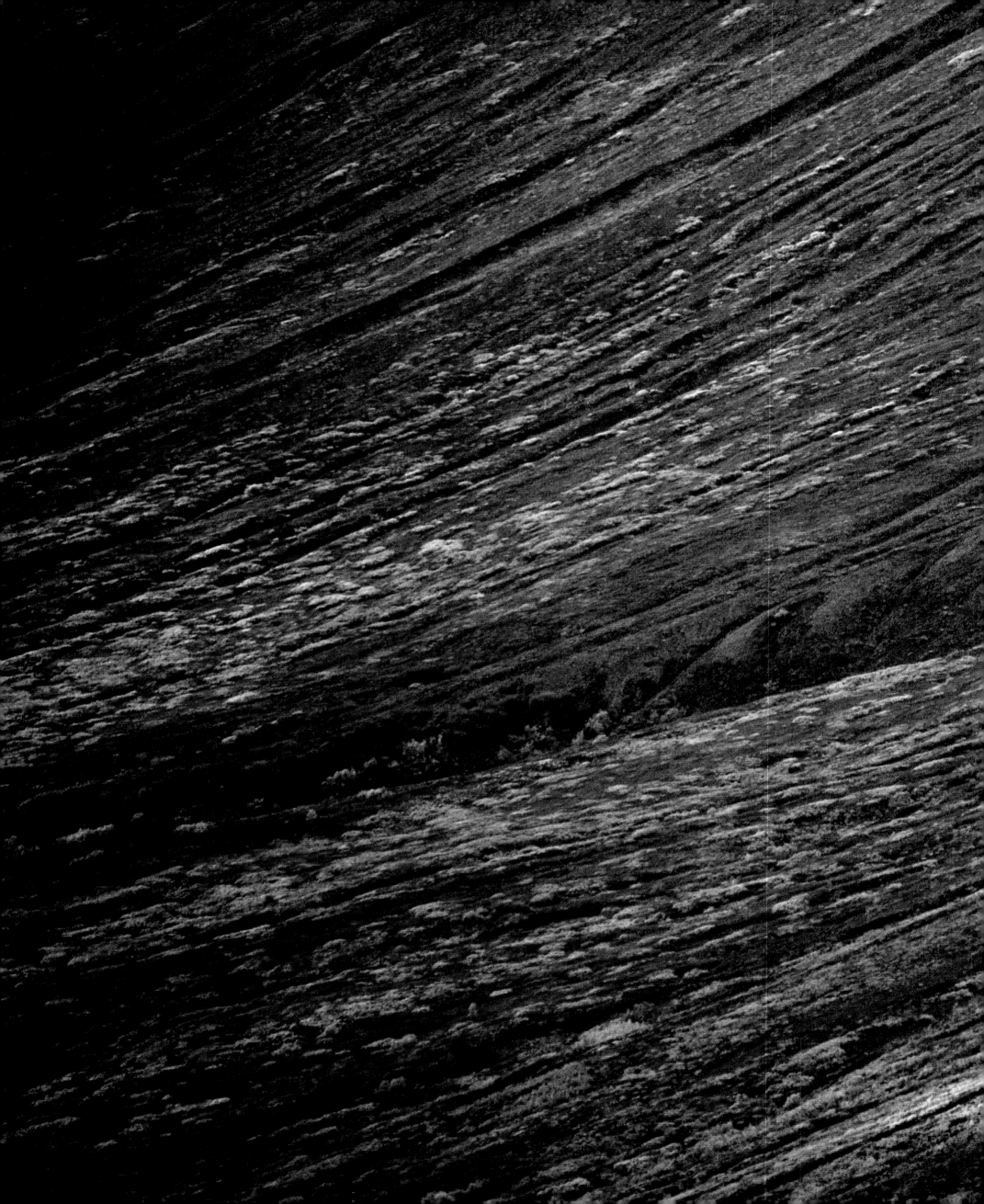

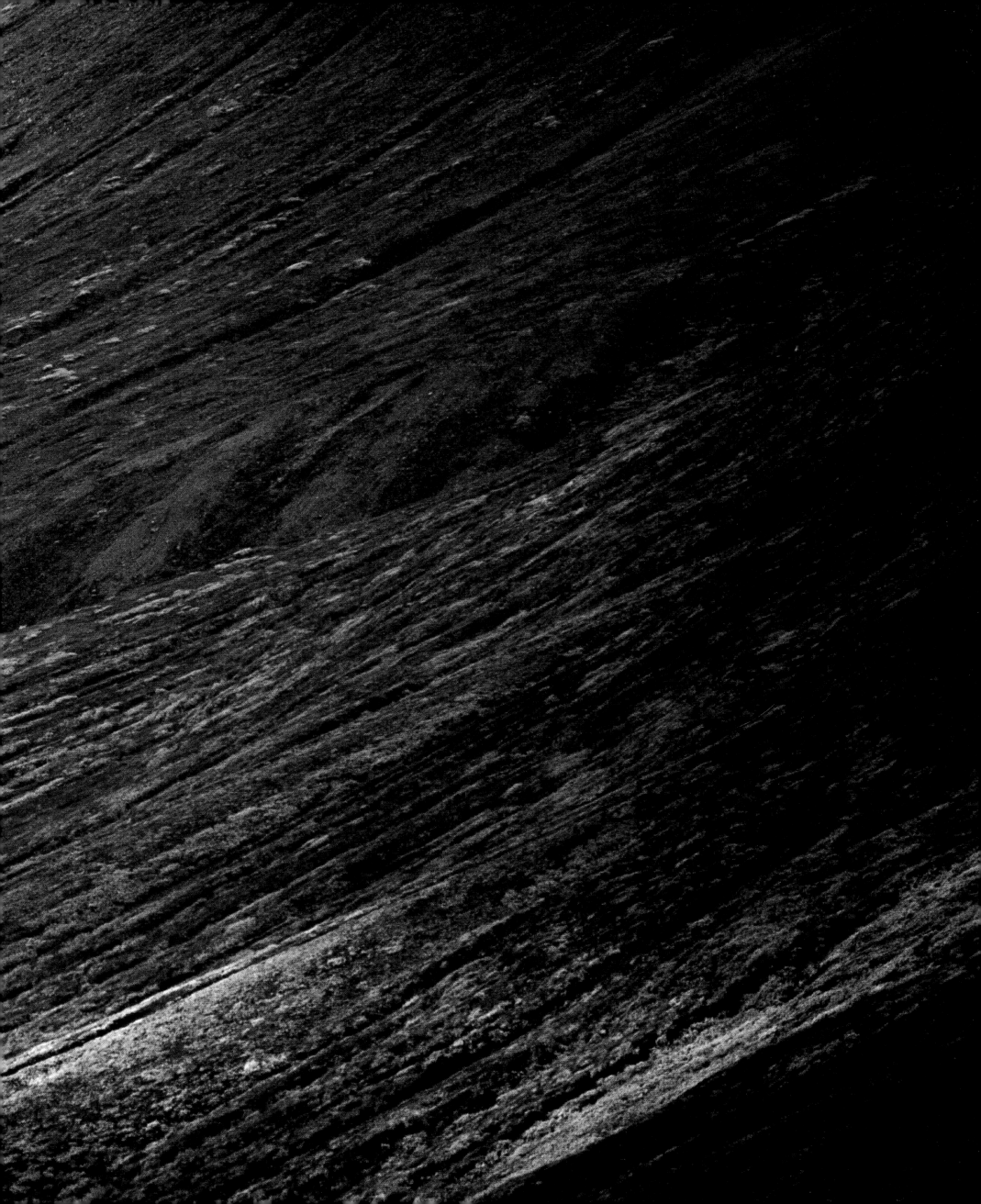

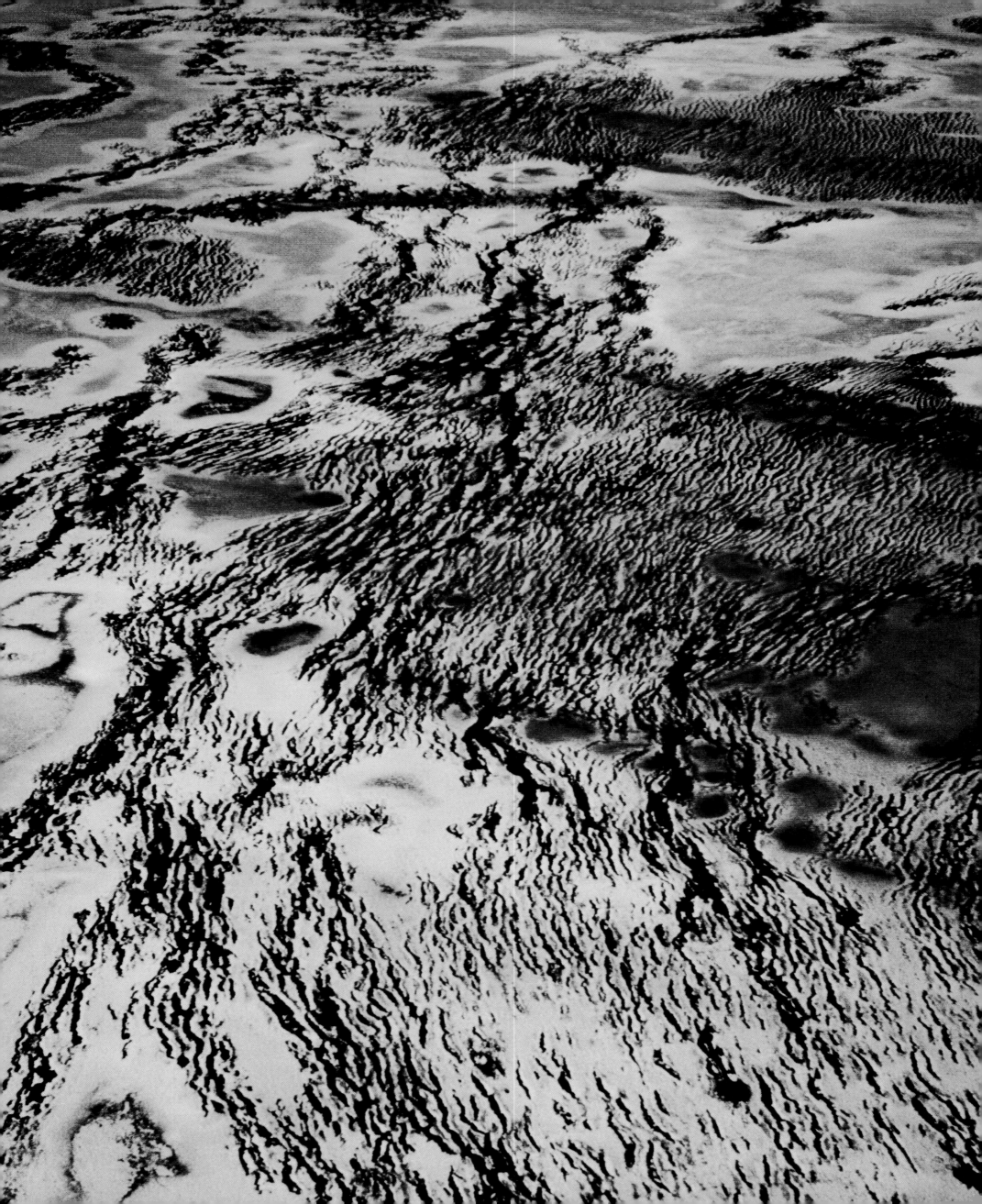

The simple idea of looking for the past in the present grew into a challenging photographic undertaking that extended over several years. My mission to capture images of nature that could evoke time and origins required lots of research and planning. I wanted to apply both new scientific ideas to my subjects and new photographic techniques to my images. On location, that often meant exposing cameras to all kinds of extremes.

Stromatolites challenged me to visualize a world from three billion years ago, back before the sky was blue. I worked by twilight and moonlight, which required long exposures sometimes extended even more with specialized neutral density filters. To photograph an erupting volcano in Hawaii, I had to use a different kind of filter—for myself. I wore a respirator against the caustic fumes that corrode camera parts and lungs alike. Film can buckle in the heat near an eruption, and when it rains, water mixes with volcanic gases in the air and comes down as diluted battery acid. I tried to keep my gear covered, but in the end, when the lava flowed, I chose for photos rather than keeping cameras safe.

Fieldwork isn't always a struggle. In the warm waters of the Great Barrier Reef, I used a rig which on land was heavy and cumbersome: a digital Nikon camera with a Light and Motion housing with two strobes on articulated arms. Underwater it became a weightless window into a world of fluid motion, as I floated around coral reefs searching for early forms of marine life.

Aerial photography is a high-speed juggling act that involves coordinating photographic opportunities with the movements of a plane—and making decisions fast. Working from the cramped space of an open Supercub, I attached gyros to my cameras to stabilize them as the pilot flew low through the turbulent air of Alaska's wilderness valleys. With diatoms, by contrast, I had all the time in the world. I photographed these minuscule organisms on specimen slides the size of a fingernail using a polarizing light microscope to which I attached a camera body. I experimented with different filters and settings to achieve an impressionistic rather than a scientific rendition. Some of my exposures were so long that I could break for lunch while the camera recorded an image.

All the images for this book were made with 35mm Nikon cameras. My camera bodies included a Nikon F6 for film capture, and a D2X, a D1, and a D100 for digital capture. I used Nikkor zoom lenses that gave me a continuous range of focal lengths, from a 12–24mm, to a 28–70 mm, a 70–200mm, and a 200–400mm, with 1.4x and 2x teleconverters. I employed Nikon Speedlight strobes to add light to situations that needed it.

My camera kit now includes an Apple MacBook Pro laptop with editing software and external hard drives for storing images I download in the field. Digital capture has altered the way I work on location, enabling me to work out solutions to technical problems on the spot. But while it was exciting to see the translation of ideas into images in real time, it was even more rewarding to experience for myself the living wonder of horseshoe crabs, stromatolites, giant tortoises, and others—the subjects who had lured me on my journey through time.

LEFT TO RIGHT: Frans Lanting with a red kangaroo in Australia; Frans Lanting and Chris Eckstrom on the rim of an active volcano, Hawaii (© Brad Lewis); Frans Lanting photographing an erupting volcano, Hawaii (© Brad Lewis); Chris Eckstrom observing early life in Yellowstone; Chris Eckstrom in camp in the Okavango Delta, Botswana; Frans Lanting with giant tortoises in the Galápagos Islands

IMAGE INDEX

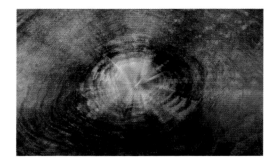

Petrified Wood, Arizona, Private Collection, p. 1
The journey of life starts in space. I wanted to create an image that visualizes the birth of the universe as described by the Big Bang theory, when matter, energy, space, and time came into being 13.7 billion years ago. I found a reflection of this cosmic event in a small slice of petrified wood. Zooming out from its surface during the exposure created an impression of an expanding universe.

Volcano at Night, Hawaii Volcanoes National Park, Hawaii, pp. 2–3
Heat within Earth makes volcanoes erupt, exhaling gases into the sky. The glow of a lava lake inside an erupting volcano illuminates fumes rising into the night sky. Volcanic gases containing carbon dioxide, nitrogen, and water vapor became the main ingredients of Earth's early atmosphere more than four billion years ago. I made this photograph after dark to emphasize the clouds of gases, which are much less apparent by day.

Moonrise over Mineral Terraces, Yellowstone National Park, Wyoming, pp. 4–5
The Moon is closer. Things are different. There are places on Earth that can take you back to a time before there was life. I went to Yellowstone's hot springs and at twilight I positioned myself to capture the Moon rising above a landscape of steaming mineral terraces. In the days of early Earth more than four billion years ago, the Moon was closer than it is today. Using a telephoto lens had the optical effect of making the Moon appear larger relative to the rest of the scene.

Stromatolites, Shark Bay, Western Australia, pp. 6–7
They alter the atmosphere, creating a breath for all life thereafter. Stromatolites are living reefs made by cyanobacteria, the microorganisms that released oxygen into the atmosphere and began to change the course of life on Earth as early as three billion years ago. Long before animals and plants evolved, stromatolites lined the shallow seas of the world. I traveled to the only place where they still occur in significant numbers, a remote lagoon in Western Australia. To evoke their ancient nature I avoided photographing them by daylight, because the sky was not yet blue when stromatolites first formed. Working at dusk gave me the low light that suggests a scene from the dawn of time. I applied neutral density filters for a time exposure of several minutes, which blurred the water and softened references to anything but the stromatolites themselves.

Moon Jellies, Monterey Bay Aquarium, California, *Aurelia labiata,* pp. 8–9
Shallow seas nurture life early on, as it grows into more complex forms. Perhaps the first creatures to have muscles, which help them pulse, and nerves, which help them sense, jellies today are living links to ancient seas of nearly 600 million years ago, when animal life was just beginning to take shape. The swaying motion of these moon jellies mesmerized me as I waited for the right moment to capture their otherworldly beauty.

Water Lilies, Okavango Delta, Botswana, *Nymphaea nouchali,* pp. 10–11
Water lilies are among the first. In a wetland in the middle of an African desert, water lilies spread their leaves to absorb light from the sun. Water lilies are among the oldest families of flowering plants living today. They drew me in as symbols of life made possible by water and sunlight. I slowly sank to the bottom of the swamp with my camera encased in an underwater housing, and from that perspective I was able to create an image of the exuberance of life.

Quiver Trees, Richtersveld National Park, South Africa, *Aloe dichotoma,* pp. 12–13
On land life turns tough. Life had to harden to minimize water loss on land. Quiver trees, succulent plants in the aloe family, thrive in arid parts of southern Africa, and cope with less than three inches of annual rainfall. I emphasized the harshness of the scene by framing a rocky background behind the trees, instead of blue sky.

Giant Tortoises in Pond, Alcedo Volcano, Galápagos Islands, *Geochelone elephantopus,* pp. 14–15
It takes time for life to break away from water. The Galápagos Islands provide a window on time. In a geologic sense the islands are young, yet they appear prehistoric. The largest animals native to this famed archipelago are giant tortoises, which can live for more than a century. These are the creatures that provided Charles Darwin with the flash of imagination that led to his theory of evolution. Today their populations are reduced on most islands. But inside the Alcedo volcano I experienced a world where giant tortoises still roamed in ancient abundance. One misty morning when the tortoises were asleep in a pond, I was able to create an image that evokes the era when reptiles dominated life on land.

Marine Iguanas and Brown Pelican, Galápagos Islands, *Amblyrhynchus cristatus* and *Pelecanus occidentalis,* pp.16–17
Some dragons from the past are still alive today. Impending doom can be imagined in this scene of reptilian forms against a brooding sky. Sixty-five million years ago an asteroid hit the Earth and caused shock waves of global extinction. The impact marked the end of an age defined by large reptiles on land, in water, and in the sky. In this image dinosaurs and pterosaurs are echoed by the silhouettes of marine iguanas and the shape of a brown pelican passing overhead.

Boulders and Surf, Hawaii Volcanoes National Park, Hawaii, p. 20
We are molded by the same force. The Moon's gravity tugs at Earth's oceans, creating tides that shape the borders of land and sea. The Moon itself was formed of material blasted from Earth when a planetary body the size of Mars crashed into Earth 4.5 billion years ago. The impact hurled rocky debris into Earth's orbit that coalesced to become the Moon, whose own gravitational force causes the ocean's tidal pulse. A time exposure of waves washing around boulders on a volcanic beach in Hawaii blurs the edges of land and water, just as has happened over time.

ELEMENTS

Lava River, Hawaii Volcanoes National Park, Hawaii, p. 28
An incandescent river of lava surges across a landscape of black basalt during a nighttime eruption at Pu'u 'O'o, the active vent of Hawaii's Kilauea volcano.

Sandstone, Utah, Private Collection, p. 30
Solidifying into spheres fueled by fire . . . In its earliest phase 4.5 billion years ago, Earth was fueled by heat from within while its surface was melted by continuous meteorite bombardments from outer space. Heavy elements sank to its core while lighter materials floated to the surface. The very lightest elements, hydrogen and helium, formed an unstable first atmosphere, which dissipated into space. The patterns of iron and manganese in this piece of sandstone made me imagine an Earth in the making.

Cooling Lava, Hawaii Volcanoes National Park, Hawaii, p. 31
Once fire gives way, Earth emerges. This primeval process is perpetuated at the edge of a lava flow, where fire retreats into the cracks beneath a rapidly cooling surface hardening into dark rock.

Sun and Volcanic Fumes, Hawaii Volcanoes National Park, Hawaii, pp. 32–33
But this is an alien planet. Sunlight barely penetrates the heavy sulfurous fumes rising from a volcanic cinder cone, where I had to wear a respirator to filter caustic gases poisonous to my lungs. Earth's early atmosphere was composed of similar gaseous exhalations released by volcanoes around the world.

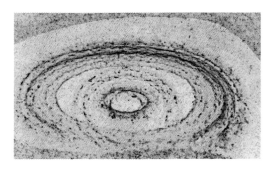

Jasper, Oregon, Private Collection, p. 35
In museums and private collections I searched for evocative patterns in rocks that could represent events that occurred during the birth of the Earth. This piece of polished jasper reminded me of an early Earth with a molten surface.

Sandstone, South Africa, Private Collection, p. 36 (top)
Energy becomes matter, turning into shapes over time. Elliptical swirls in a piece of sandstone evoke matter spinning around the Sun as the solar system was forming.

Rhyolite, Utah, Private Collection, p. 36 (bottom)
A cross-section of volcanic rhyolite suggested to me a scene from early Earth with billowing plumes of gas and layers of solidifying rock.

Jasper, Oregon, Private Collection, p. 37
I envisioned the fractured crust of an Earth forged by tectonic forces in this small piece of jasper.

Volcano Erupting, Hawaii Volcanoes National Park, Hawaii, p. 38
A time exposure of several seconds traces the expulsion of red-hot rock from a spatter cone inside the crater of Pu'u 'O'o.

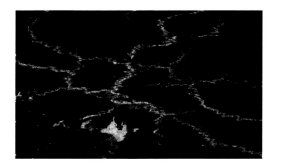

Lava Lake, Hawaii Volcanoes National Park, Hawaii, pp. 40–41
This planet is restless; it roils inside. One evening when I watched rafts of molten rock slide past one another in a lava lake inside Pu'u 'O'o's crater, it was like seeing the movements of continental plates floating atop the liquid interior of the Earth. Deep inside Earth, magma churns in huge convection currents that push continents across its surface, causing earthquakes and volcanic activity where the plates grind against each other or where they tear apart.

Cooling Lava Flow, Hawaii Volcanoes National Park, Hawaii, pp. 42–43
A landscape of cooling lava steams in the morning sun. To walk across a fresh lava flow I had to plan every step to avoid punching through the upper crust. Heat rose through my boots when I paused; I couldn't put my camera gear down for long. Even though it looked solid at the surface, I knew there was liquid lava right underneath.

Volcano at Dawn, Hawaii Volcanoes National Park, Hawaii, pp. 44–45
One morning when I climbed to the rim of Pu'u 'O'o, the lava lake inside the crater had formed a thin gray crust, but spatter cones were still glowing and fumes were rising from cracks in the fractured landscape. I felt like I had walked into a scene from the dawn of time. This was an Earth in motion just as it was around 4.4 billion years ago when its surface was solidifying.

Geyser at Night, Rotorua, New Zealand, p. 46
Geysers vent steam. On early Earth, geysers blew jets of boiling water and steam into the atmosphere for many millions of years, adding to the water vapor released by volcanoes. I waited near an erupting geyser until nighttime to create an impression of this primordial exhalation of water from Earth's interior.

Headlands in Surf, Monterey Bay, California, p. 47
Under a rainy evening sky when it was almost too dark to see, my camera caught sea mist and surf swirling around coastal headlands in a scene that hints at the time when Earth's oceans formed.

Falling Water, Iguaçu National Park, Brazil, pp. 48–49
When Earth cools, rain falls for eons, giving birth to oceans. After meteorite bombardments began to subside more than four billion years ago, Earth cooled, and water vapor that had saturated the early atmosphere condensed into torrential rains that lasted for millions of years. Over time water inundated the Earth and created a first global ocean. By positioning myself at the base of a thundering waterfall, I was able to create an image in which Earth has all but disappeared, buried beneath an avalanche of water.

Salt Streaks on Mud Flats, Makgadikgadi Pans, Botswana, p. 50
Streaks of salt foam blown by the wind from an alkaline lake fan across the drying mud flats of the Makgadikgadi Pans in the heart of the Kalahari Desert. To me this desolate scene was a step toward imagining the fate of Mars, a planet that once had water on its surface. Some scientists theorize that on Mars, ultraviolet light from the Sun split water into lightweight hydrogen, which floated into space, and oxygen, which combined with iron to form the oxides that make that planet red.

Moon over Salt Desert, Makgadikgadi Pans, Botswana, p. 51
When water vanishes, Earth becomes like Mars. One evening I stood in a lifeless salt desert from which all water had disappeared. It was so eerily silent that I could hear the blood beat in my own ears as I watched a distant Moon rising above the blue hues of Earth's shadow against a pink evening sky.

Erosion Patterns, Canyonlands National Park, Utah, pp. 52–53
The low-slanting light of a cold winter sunrise illuminates patterns water has carved into the naked surface of the Earth, just as it has done since the first landmasses began to emerge from Earth's global ocean around three billion years ago.

Icescape, Patriot Hills, Antarctica, pp. 54–55
Water freezes around the Poles. In its early history Earth experienced at least two extended cold periods known as "Snowball Earth" episodes. Most of the planet's surface became encased in ice and oceans froze to depths of up to half a mile. A scene from the icy interior of Antarctica today visualizes these eras of extreme cold.

Icicles and Sun, Alta Bay, Antarctica, p. 56
Water is a key to life, but in frozen form it is a latent force. Icicles dripping from an iceberg stranded on the edge of Antarctica reminded me of the fine line between liquid water and ice, and point to the narrow margins for life itself.

Water and Mud Flats, Copper River Delta, Alaska, p. 57
Water shapes the edges of the Earth. It erodes mountains, carries sediments to the sea, and forms mudflats that glint, backlit by the sun, on a rising tide.

Glacier and Mountains, Wrangell-St. Elias National Park, Alaska, pp. 58–59
Earth and water interact on a grand scale where the Malaspina Glacier slowly grinds past the Wrangell Mountains, pushing lines of rocky sediments crushed from the rugged slopes by the pressure and movement of ice. At an altitude of 17,000 feet I shot through an open window of a small plane to get an overview of this gigantic river of ice.

Water Reflections, Biesbosch, Netherlands, p. 60
Liquid water is the essential medium for life on Earth, and there is virtually no water on Earth without life. From a small boat floating on a summer lake I captured the sensuous swirls of water reflecting a blue sky without revealing any of the life that is nurtured within.

Boiling Mud, Rotorua, New Zealand, p. 61
Perched precariously at the slippery edge of a hot spring filled with boiling mud heated from deep within the Earth, I captured an erupting fountain of mud, an energized mix of four elements—earth, air, fire, and water.

Grand Prismatic Spring, Yellowstone National Park, Wyoming, p. 62
Life arises around cracks in the Earth. From a helicopter hovering over a hot spring, patterns of early life became apparent to me when I saw how cyanobacteria tainted the edges of the spring brown. Other single-celled organisms live in the near-boiling blue water in the center, invisible to the naked eye. Most of these are archaea, whose name means "ancient ones." Many of them thrive in extreme environments similar to those where life may have begun on Earth as early as four billion years ago.

Ediacaran Fossil, Australian Museum, Sydney, *Tribrachidium heraldicum,* p.64
Ediacaran organisms are only known from faint imprints in rocks dating back around 600 million years. Named for the hills in southern Australia where they were first found, these fossils constitute the earliest confirmed record of multicellular animal life. The shapes of some suggest affinities with jellies and worms, but others, like this spiraling form with triple symmetry, appear unrelated to any other known life-forms.

Diatom, Farlow Herbarium, Harvard University, Massachusetts, p. 65
Life needs a membrane to contain itself. The boundaries of the first living cells may have been simply a layer of oily molecules which separated life from its environment. To me this diatom's circular shape symbolized the membrane that was a prerequisite to the evolution of the first living things.

Geyser at Dawn, Nevada, pp. 66–67
Where that energy touches water, a new element appears: Life. A momentary flash from my strobe illuminates the green filaments of cyanobacteria growing on the dome of a geyser spewing boiling water into a morning sky. The mix of chemical and environmental conditions found at hot springs and geysers on Earth's surface and at deep-sea vents on the ocean floor has led many scientists to believe that life may have originally evolved in similar places on early Earth.

Bacterial Mats, Kronotsky State Biosphere Reserve, Kamchatka, Russia, pp. 68–69
Mud and minerals become substrates where life begins to multiply, thickening in places . . . I traveled to a remote river valley in Kamchatka to create impressions of Earth's first ecosystems. In a geothermal wilderness of hissing fumaroles and spouting geysers, I focused on a rocky panorama of multicolored bacteria of many different species; they formed slimy mats on a boulder-studded slope where near-boiling water from a hot spring cascaded into a near-freezing freshwater stream. Along such temperature gradients, single-celled organisms developed into interdependent communities long before plants or animals existed.

Stromatolites at Twilight, Shark Bay, Western Australia, p. 70
. . . growing structures under a primeval sky. In the stillness of twilight glowing in a cloudless sky, I felt transported back to a time when nothing moved except waves lapping against the mounds of ancient stromatolites. The sky's burnished color suggests an atmosphere when it contained virtually no oxygen.

Stromatolites at Dawn, Shark Bay, Western Australia, pp. 72–73
Low tide at sunrise exposes the cracked domes of stromatolites lining the shores of Shark Bay. The surfaces of these mounds are the newest sediment layers formed by living communities of cyanobacteria. As early as three billion years ago the ancestors of these microorganisms began to release the oxygen that altered Earth's atmosphere and created conditions favorable for the evolution of complex life. The spreading pink clouds of sunrise hint at a change in the air.

Fossil Stromatolites, Bolivia, Private Collection, p. 74
A cross-section of two-billion-year-old fossilized stromatolites found in the Andes reveals their laminated structure. On the surface of a stromatolite mound, cyanobacteria secrete calcium carbonate, which combines with mud and sediments to form a new layer. Over time the mounds grow, but slowly. A stromatolite mound three feet high could be 2,000 years old.

Banded Iron, Hammersley Range, Australia, Private Collection, p. 75
A breath that became fossilized as iron. Twisted bands of bright-red oxidized iron deposited more than two billion years ago in Western Australia are evidence of a momentous change on Earth. They formed when massive amounts of oxygen produced by cyanobacteria combined with dissolved iron in Earth's oceans. The seas began to rust. Iron oxides rained down to the ocean floor and were compressed into sedimentary layers that in places such as Australia's Hammersley Range are up to a mile thick. As I photographed this slab of banded iron, I was struck by the irony that the iron ore so essential for the construction of the machines that power modern human societies owes its origins to ancient bacterial processes.

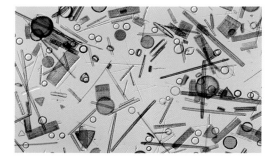

Diatoms, Farlow Herbarium, Harvard University, Massachusetts, pp. 76–77
Life replicates and mutates. An assortment of diatoms from a sample of seawater photographed through a microscope reveals the kaleidoscopic geometry of their forms. They are the silica skeletons of single-celled algae that flourish everywhere in fresh and salt water, but are so tiny that 25 million would fit in a teaspoon. Algae are ancient; they emerged perhaps as early as 1.8 billion years ago. Diatoms evolved much more recently, and they are now so abundant that they account for up to one quarter of all photosynthetic activity on the planet. More than 70,000 species have been recognized so far.

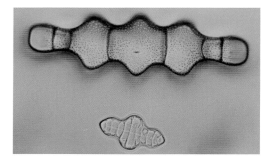

Diatoms, Farlow Herbarium, Harvard University, Massachusetts, *Terpsinoe musica* (top) and *Tetracyclus lacustris* (bottom), p. 78
I spent a week in a windowless basement office at Harvard University, searching for specimens in its diatom collection. Each specimen slide is smaller than a fingernail, but can hold thousands of diatoms. I reviewed them through the eyepiece of a microscope and immersed myself in a world I never knew existed. The colorless skeletons of these diatoms are made of glassy silica. By applying polarized light, colored filters, and selective focus, I was able to create images that bring to mind the complex processes of multicellular life. To me these individual diatoms of two separate species embodied the idea of change and mutation.

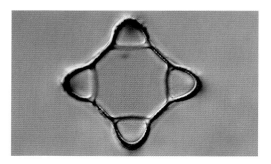

Diatom, Farlow Herbarium, Harvard University, Massachusetts, *Trinacria exsculpta,* p. 79 (top)
I adjusted my focus on this four-sided fossil diatom to evoke the elegant symmetry of cell division.

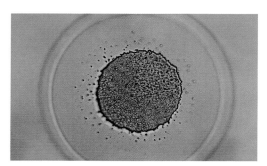

Diatom, Farlow Herbarium, Harvard University, Massachusetts, *Hyalodiscus subtilis,* p. 79 (bottom)
In the silica skeleton of this marine diatom I found a representation of the mysterious beauty of the single cell, with a nucleus surrounded by a watery membrane.

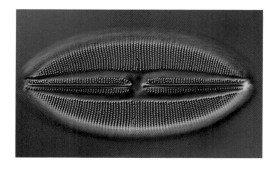

Diatom, Farlow Herbarium, Harvard University, Massachusetts, *Lyrella lyra,* pp. 80–81
I chose intensely colored filters to photograph the patterns of this futuristic-looking diatom. Its scientific name speaks to the elongated H-shaped center, which resembles a lyre.

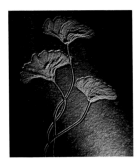

Fossil Sea Lilies, Germany, Private Collection, p. 82
Life evolves when light and oxygen increase. These fossilized sea lilies, or crinoids, look like flowers, but they are actually the imprints of animals known as echinoderms which began to evolve around 525 million years ago. The five-sided body plan that distinguishes modern echinoderms such as starfish and sea urchins first appeared in crinoids some 20 million years later. They became so abundant that vast areas of ancient seas turned into gardens of swaying sea lilies, attached to the sea floor with stalks, some rising as high as 70 feet.

Flower Hat Jelly, Monterey Bay Aquarium, California, *Olindias formosa,* p. 83
Life learns to move. I was spellbound when I saw the multicolored tentacles wave from the pin-striped bell of this extraordinary flower hat jelly, a drifter in sea currents which also spends time moving along the ocean floor. The ancestors of jellies were among the first animals whose bodies exhibited an organized architecture, with groups of cells joined together as tissues that performed unified functions.

Crystal Jelly, Monterey Bay Aquarium, California, *Aequorea victoria,* p. 84
Nearly transparent and with a body that is 95 percent water, a crystal jelly glows blue when light-producing organs around the rim of its umbrella luminesce. It trails long tentacles with stinging cells as it pulses through the water. Like all jellies this one is a carnivore, and can expand its bell to swallow other jellies.

Comb Jelly, Monterey Bay Aquarium, California, *Mnemiopsis leidyi,* p. 85
Rainbow colors pulse from a comb jelly as light passes through its rows of rippling combs, specialized cells that help it move through the water.

Fossil Ammonoid, Solnhofen, Germany, *Lithacoceras* sp., p. 86
The spiraling shape of a fossilized ammonoid shell shows the sectioned air chambers once used by a living ammonoid to control its buoyancy in the sea. Ammonoids became major hunters around 400 million years ago, using air-filled chambers and jet propulsion to get around. Their body plan was so successful that they proliferated into many forms, from thumb-size discs to giants 15 feet long.

Nautilus Shell, South Pacific Ocean, Private Collection, *Nautilus* sp., p. 87
A cross-section of a nautilus shell shows the same air chambers used to move up and down in the water column as were employed by their now-extinct ammonoid relatives. Nautiluses today are the sole survivors of this formidable lineage of marine predators. By day they hide in deep water to escape predation by fish, and by night they rise to pursue prey in shallow water, when fish sleep.

Fossil Trilobite, Ontario, Canada, Private Collection, *Gabriceraurus dentatus,* p. 88
Life begins to see. The first eyes grew on trilobites which began to flourish around 525 million years ago during a period marked by the abrupt appearance of so many new forms of life that it became known as the Cambrian Explosion. Some trilobites were crawlers or burrowers, others became swimmers; the body armor of this trilobite may have been a response to predators such as ammonoids. Trilobites developed compound eyes with multiple lenses that were sensitive to motion and became important assets in predator detection. A few possessed eyes so huge they were capable of 360-degree vision. This trilobite specimen had been so exquisitely prepared by a master fossil carver that the raised bumps of its two compound eyes are visible in great detail, and I could almost imagine it moving off the rock that had encased it for many millions of years.

Fossil Coral, Indonesia, Private Collection, p. 89
Life hardens and becomes defensive. A slice through a piece of fossilized coral reveals the common defense and communal lifestyle of polyps that built coral reefs. The first reefs built by multicellular animals appeared in Ediacaran seas approximately 550 million years ago.

Coral Polyps Feeding, Great Barrier Reef, Australia, *Sarcophyton* sp., p. 90
As incoming tidal currents sweep across coral heads on a shallow reef surrounding Heron Island, I drifted above them; with my camera encased in an underwater housing and two strobes attached to either side to reveal details, I focused on the masses of tiny polyps extending tentacles to filter nutrients from the water.

Staghorn Coral, Great Barrier Reef, Australia, *Acropora millepora,* p. 91 (top)
The spiky tips of staghorn coral reach toward the surface of the sea. Coral polyps hidden inside support photosynthetic algae in their tissues. Although the polyps capture plankton from seawater, the algae provide most of the nutrients the coral polyps need to grow and produce limestone. In turn, the polyps shelter the algae, and themselves, inside the limestone reef structures they build with their secretions.

Sea Cucumber, Great Barrier Reef, Australia, *Stichopus variegatus,* p. 91 (bottom)
Lying flat on the bottom of a shallow lagoon I stared at a creature that is hard to fathom. Sea cucumbers are bottom dwellers who make up 90 percent of the biomass of the deep ocean floor. Inside its cylinder shape hides an animal with no brain, no eyes, and no backbone. It looks like a swollen worm, but it's actually a spiny-skinned echinoderm with an elongated version of their characteristic five-sided body plan. Sea cucumbers crawl using rows of tube feet along their bodies, and shovel in decaying matter using adapted feet at one end. When in danger, they can confuse predators by expelling most of their internal organs, which later regenerate.

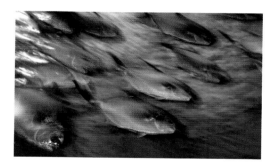

Snub-nosed Darts, Sydney Aquarium, Australia, *Trachinotus blochi,* pp. 92–93
A school of snub-nosed darts shoots through water in unison. By panning my camera along with them while my strobe fired, I created a sense of their quicksilvery motion. The first jawed fish appeared in Devonian seas some 425 million years ago. Their internal skeletons built around a flexible backbone were a major innovation that enabled them to emerge as a new lineage of predators. These snub-nosed darts also possess powerful bones in their throats for crushing the shells of mollusks on which they feed, giving them the nickname of "oyster crackers."

OUT OF THE SEA

Leatherback Sea Turtle Tracks, Galibi National Reserve, Surinam, *Dermochelys coriacea,* p. 94
The lone tracks of a sea turtle who had come ashore on a tropical beach made me think of a time around 400 million years ago when dry land was still an evolutionary frontier. Life faced new challenges on land: It required body support, it had to avoid drying out, and it needed to adapt to breathing in air.

Fossil Eurypterids, New York, Private Collection, *Eurypterus remipes,* p. 96
Creatures of nightmares appeared in the seas 480 million years ago. They were sea scorpions who became the most fearsome predators of their time. Some of them grew up to nine feet long. Those sea monsters lived in the same region of the eastern United States where these smaller eurypterid fossils were found. Halfway around the world, I scrambled down into a deep canyon in Western Australia to see fossilized eurypterid tracks crossing rock that was once a tidal flat, indicating that eventually a few of them ventured onto land.

Sally Lightfoot Crabs, Galápagos Islands, *Grapsus grapsus,* p. 97
Like the sea scorpions of the past, these modern crabs are arthropods—animals with an exoskeleton and jointed legs—and that gives them a hold on land as they cling to an intertidal rock in the Galápagos.

Horseshoe Crabs Spawning, Delaware Bay, New Jersey, *Limulus polyphemus,* p. 98
Among the first to leave the sea, they still do what they've done for ages. One spring evening I waded into the shallow water of Delaware Bay, and with horseshoe crabs crawling over my bare feet, I captured the timeless ritual of their spawning.

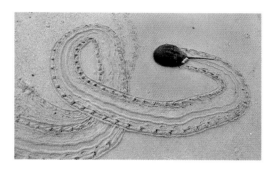

Horseshoe Crab, Delaware Bay, New Jersey, *Limulus polyphemus,* pp. 100–101
Horseshoe crabs are equipped with several pairs of compound eyes, and they can see both underwater and on land. But one morning when I went back to the beach where I had witnessed a nocturnal orgy of mass spawning under a full moon, I found one individual crab turning circles in the sand, seemingly unsure of which way led back to the sea.

Sally Lightfoot Crab, Galápagos Islands, *Grapsus grapsus,* pp. 102–103
If species count matters, then arthropods possess the most successful animal body plan on Earth today. More than 80 percent of all living species of animals are arthropods, which means "jointed legs." This huge group includes all insects, spiders, and crustaceans. What arthropods share besides jointed legs is a hard exoskeleton which originally armored them against marine predators, but this protection also served arthropods very well for an existence out of the water.

Scorpion, Kalahari Desert, Botswana, *Opistophthalmus* sp., p. 104
Scorpions follow prey out of the sea. The scorpion that scurried around my camp in the Kalahari one night was a tiny relative of the once-mighty eurypterids, but the threat of its poisonous stinger was enough to make me back off. Scorpions became pioneers on land as early as 400 million years ago and ultimately some of them adapted to life in deserts, while their marine ancestors all faded away.

Spider Web, Monterey Bay, California, p. 105
Dewdrops on a spider web I found in a meadow near my home one summer morning turned into twinkling orbs of light when I photographed the web with a macro lens set at a shallow focus. As ephemeral as spider webs may seem, they have a long history. The webs themselves have left no mark, but the tiny organ on a spider's body from which it spins out silk has been identified on a fossil 420 million years old.

Lichen Landscape, Falkland Islands, pp. 106–107
They cling to rock and transform barren land. The lichens covering rocks surrounding my campsite on a blustery island in the South Atlantic are the result of a partnership between fungi and algae that was forged in a distant past. Alone, neither of these organisms with aquatic origins could survive on bare rock but together they have colonized the most extreme environments on Earth, ranging from deserts to polar regions, and they started doing this more than 400 million years ago, when dry land was still uninhabited.

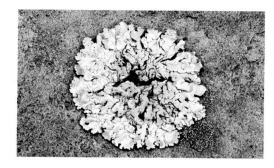

Lichen, Vermilion Cliffs National Monument, Arizona, p. 108

Lichens develop as a co-op: Fungi marry algae. When the fungi in a lichen partnership attach themselves to rocks, they extract mineral nutrients and give shelter to the algae living inside them; the algae conduct photosynthesis and provide the fungi with sugars in a mutually beneficial relationship known as symbiosis. For me personally, it was humbling to see something so simple that has survived the ages.

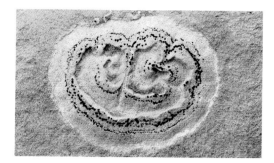

Lichen Scar, Vermilion Cliffs National Monument, Arizona, p. 109 (top)

Acids produced by the fungus partner in a lichen etch the rock beneath it and slowly break it down. When a lichen dies, it leaves behind a blister on the rock.

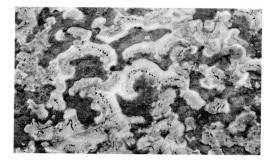

Lichen Scars, Vermilion Cliffs National Monument, Arizona, p. 109 (bottom)

Most lichens grow very slowly, in some cases just a fraction of an inch in a century. Some individual lichens may be several thousand years old, making them among the oldest living things on Earth. But even for lichens there are limits to life, and these blisters left on sandstone by lichens now withered away looked to me like inscriptions of time.

Whisk Fern, Hawaii Volcanoes National Park, Hawaii, *Psilotum nudum,* pp. 110–111

True land plants arise, leafless at first. On a lava flow in Hawaii I crouched down in front of a tiny whisk fern that had sprouted in a crack, colonizing land just as the first land plants did as early as 470 million years ago. With their simple, branching shapes, whisk ferns look like those pioneers, and just like them, they don't have leaves or roots; photosynthesis takes place in their stems.

False Staghorn Ferns, Hawaii Volcanoes National Park, Hawaii, *Dicranopteris linearis,* p. 112

The fundamental forms of ferns follow . . . Ferns have been uncurling fiddleheads for 370 million years. Their stems serve as conduits for an internal plumbing system of vascular tissue that early plants like ferns, club mosses, and horsetails evolved—a major innovation that helped plants transport water and nutrients and develop the rigid structure they needed to grow upright out of water.

Filmy Fern, Westland National Park, New Zealand, *Hymenophyllum dilatatum,* p. 113

. . . bearing spores that foreshadow seeds. The translucent leaves of filmy ferns are just one cell layer thick, and can only thrive in dripping-wet environments. The spores that are encased at the leaf tips need water as well to complete their reproductive cycle.

Club Moss, Hawaii Volcanoes National Park, Hawaii, *Lycopodium cernuum,* p. 114

Once they learn to stay upright, they grow in size and shape. Around 380 million years ago, club mosses had solved the problem of building a rigid structure that allowed for extended vertical growth, and they turned into trees more than 150 feet tall. They formed vast forests in swamps where their scaly straight trunks stood only a few feet apart. That era is gone, but when I came upon a miniature version of these prehistoric giants near a steam vent on the slopes of a volcano, I laid down flat on the ground so I could capture the former glory of their tree crowns.

Southern Bull Kelp in Tide Pool, Falkland Islands, *Durvillaea antarctica,* p. 115 (top)
Kelp forms swaying forests in cool seawater where single strands of these multicellular brown algae can reach up to 200 feet in length. But because it lacks a rigid internal structure, kelp is dependent on the support of water. In this tide pool on an uninhabited island in the frigid South Atlantic, I captured an image of kelp fronds swirling with the surges of the sea.

Spike Moss, Marie Selby Botanical Garden, Sarasota, Florida, *Selaginella* sp., p. 115 (bottom)
Spike mosses today are minuscule remnants of a group of plants that was once diverse and widespread more than 300 million years ago, during an era when continents were merging and at times, much of the world was covered with vast tropical swamplands.

Horsetails, Los Padres National Forest, Big Sur, California, *Equisetum* sp., pp. 116–117
Life flourishes in swamps. Looking down on a patch of horsetails that grew knee-high in a wet depression, I imagined seeing the canopy of a forest from 350 million years ago. Like club mosses, horsetails once attained great size and abundance, and their remains are important components of the massive coal beds around the world that have powered the industrial enterprises of modern human societies.

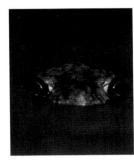

Desert Spadefoot Frog, Central Australia, *Notaden nichollsi,* p. 119
Frogs adapt to deserts. Amphibians like this desert spadefoot frog are dependent on water for reproduction, but over time they managed to colonize even harsh environments like Australia's central desert, where water is a scarce resource. The desert spadefoot frog has mastered the art of surviving without water for years. It burrows into the ground, secretes a membrane around itself, and goes into the deep sleep of aestivation. But it only takes one rainstorm to wake it up. I photographed this frog as it broke the surface of a patch of wet sand and resumed life.

Land Snail, Monterey Bay, California, p. 120
Slugs become snails. A land snail slides along on a trail of slime that smoothes its way over hard ground in my backyard. The shells of land snails have their origins in the sea, where they evolved as a defense of soft-bodied animals against predators such as eurypterids and ammonoids. Shells today help snails minimize desiccation, just as they did when these mollusks first ventured onto land.

Mudskipper, Daintree National Park, Queensland, Australia, *Periophthalmodon freycineti,* p. 121
Fish try amphibian life. Mudskippers are walking fish that live in tropical mangroves, where they have evolved an amphibious lifestyle. They can move their eyes up and down like submarine periscopes, enabling them to see above or below water as they cruise shallow tidal creeks. Their muscular pectoral fins are just as good for pushing them along on the mud as they are for swimming. Like fish, mudskippers breathe by absorbing oxygen from water through their gills. Like amphibians, mudskippers can also breathe through their skin. When they're out of the water, they carry their own internal "reverse" scuba tanks as well: Large gill chambers filled with water help keep their gills moist and oxygenated while they're ashore. As I saw them skipping along on mudflats and even climbing into mangrove trees, it was easy to imagine the evolutionary steps that led from life in the sea to life on land.

Green Sea Turtle Hatchling, Galibi National Reserve, Surinam, *Chelonia mydas,* p. 123
Moments away from the shelter that the sea provides, a green sea turtle hatchling hurries across the beach on the morning that it emerged from a nest incubated by the sun above the tide line.

277

Leatherback Sea Turtle, Galibi National Reserve, Surinam, *Dermochelys coriacea,* pp. 124–125
On a steamy tropical beach in Surinam, I watched this giant female leatherback turtle struggle when she dragged herself ashore at twilight and deposited her eggs, a process that took much of the night. In the darkness, I listened to her hiss and groan as she labored to excavate a hole with her hind flippers and bury her eggs inside, an ancient urge that sea turtles around the world have followed since the time when they first appeared, along with dinosaurs, some 230 million years ago.

ON LAND

Savanna at Dawn, Emas National Park, Brazil, p. 126
A great change rocks the Earth; continents get dry. Life on Earth was shaken up 250 million years ago during an upheaval known as the Permian Extinction. At that time, all continents had merged into one landmass called Pangaea, which stretched from Pole to Pole. The extinction may have been triggered by an asteroid impact, by extended volcanic activity, global warming, toxic levels of carbon dioxide in the sea—or a catastrophic combination of several crises. Within a relatively short period, perhaps only 160,000 years, 90 percent of all species on the planet disappeared. The great swamp forests of giant club mosses and horsetails died out, along with most of the early land reptiles, the synapsids, who had dominated for 60 million years. Climates turned arid. Deserts stretched across Pangaea's interior. Prominent among the survivors were a few hard-skinned reptiles and cone-bearing trees whose respective secrets to success were amniotic eggs and seeds. It was their descendants who would recolonize the Earth. A landscape at dawn from a dry savanna in Brazil sets the stage for this new wave of life.

Dendrite Patterns, Solnhofen, Germany, Private Collection, p. 128
The delicate pattern in this piece of sandstone intrigued me. It looks just like a fossilized plant, but it is actually a dendrite, a pseudofossil produced by minerals precipitating along fracture lines in the rock, and not by a biological process. This example of the common geometry seen in many living and nonliving things can be explained by fractal principles. Fractals are mathematically generated patterns that look the same no matter at which scale they are reproduced. They can form complex structures, many of which bear a striking resemblance to patterns in the natural world. To me, fractal patterns are a visual expression of what happens on the boundary between order and chaos; at those edges of uncertainty, evolution forges new forms over time that are the result of interactions between living organisms and their environments.

Araucaria Tree, Native to Chile, *Araucaria araucana,* p. 129
Others still grow defenses against foraging giants. Like dendrites, the repeating branching patterns of this araucaria tree illustrate principles of fractal geometry. These ancient conifers spread after the Permian Extinction when climates became more extreme and posed new challenges for life on land. The spiky leaves that spiral around the trunk and branches of this araucaria may have once helped protect its forebears against browsing by dinosaurs. Araucarias still exist in the Southern Hemisphere on the slopes of the Andes and in the forests of New Zealand, but I grew this specimen in my own garden as a personal tribute to a tough survivor.

Cycad, Kirstenbosch National Botanical Garden, Cape Town, South Africa, *Encephalartos friderici-guilielmi,* p. 131
Plants like cycads remain rock hard. I have always been drawn to cycads. With their elementary shapes they look like they've weathered the ages. Though they resemble palms or ferns, cycads are neither; it is the seeds contained in their distinctive cones that define them. Cycads are seed plants, which rose to prominence after the Permian Extinction, when the land had turned dry. Seeds shielded plant embryos inside a protective coat where they could remain dormant until conditions were suitable for germination. It was an innovation that liberated plants from dependence on water as a medium for fertilization. Scattered forests of seed plants, dominated by cycads and conifers, colonized the interior of Pangaea, with cycads preferring warmth and conifers adapting to cold. To highlight the developing cones on this mature cycad tree in a renowned botanical collection, I pressed in close with a wide-angle lens to emphasize their significance relative to the rest of the tree.

Palm Savanna, Horombe Plateau, Madagascar, pp. 132–133
Dinosaur time shimmers in parts of Madagascar and Brazil. One day when I drove on a rutted sandy track through the wide-open landscapes of Madagascar's southern plateau, I came upon this scene, a dry savanna dotted by drought-tolerant and fire-resistant palms. It made me think of the conditions that became prevalent in large parts of the Earth at the time when dinosaurs began their evolution some 230 million years ago.

Tuatara, North Brother Island, New Zealand, *Sphenodon guntheri,* pp. 134–135
Tuataras are echoes of that era. All reptiles are classified as either crocodilians, snakes and lizards, turtles and tortoises, or tuataras. In the first three groups there are thousands of living species; in the tuatara group there are only two. Tuataras are the last survivors of an ancient lineage that first shows up in the fossil record 240 million years ago. Tuataras today look practically the same, and are often referred to as living fossils. Their endurance in evolutionary time is paralleled by their individual longevity: These slow-growing dragons can live up to a century, once they emerge from eggs that take up to 15 months to hatch. Tuataras survive on just a few small islands off New Zealand. I joined researchers working on one tiny islet, the only place in the world where the rarest of the two species of tuataras lives. One evening I had the opportunity to create this portrait. Sharp side-lighting from a strobe made the tuatara look as immutable as the rock itself, a creature frozen in time.

Giant Tortoises by Moonlight, Alcedo Volcano, Galápagos Islands, *Geochelone elephantopus,* p. 136
Water still beckons all the time. Isolated places such as the Galápagos Islands provide a glimpse into the era when large reptiles dominated ecosystems on land. The giant tortoises who live at the top of Alcedo volcano spend the night in ponds because the water is warmer than the cool air on the volcano summit. I made this image in the middle of the night, by moonlight only.

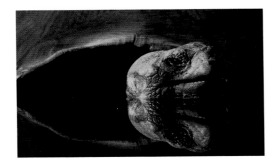

Giant Tortoise in Pond, Alcedo Volcano, Galápagos Islands, *Geochelone elephantopus,* pp. 138–139
Jaws form first, teeth come later. Giant tortoises have no teeth; they can't chew their food. They just tear it off and swallow it. Their digestive system is not very effective at extracting nutrients from whatever they eat. It takes up to three weeks for a meal to pass through a giant tortoise's guts, and at the end of it, you can often still identify the original plants the tortoise ate.

Marine Iguanas, Galápagos Islands, *Amblyrhynchus cristatus,* p. 140
Marine iguanas in the Galápagos live on a thermal knife's edge. Their main food is algae growing on rocks below the tide line, but before they can go out to forage in the cold seawater, they need to warm up. They bask in the sun to increase their body temperature and then slide into the sea to feed for a few hours. But by the time they come out, they are so sluggish they can barely crawl, and they have to bask again.

Nile Crocodile Hatchling, Okavango Delta, Botswana, *Crocodylus niloticus,* p. 141
With eggs and seeds life has a chance on land to shelter new life in the making. The egg from which this baby crocodile is hatching was the key to reptilian success on land. Eggs had evolved earlier in fish and amphibians, but reptiles mastered a new version, the amniotic egg, in which a developing embryo is protected inside a shell lined with a semi-permeable membrane that holds moisture in but allows gas exchange with the world outside. Amniotic eggs can be soft and leathery, as in lizards, turtles, crocodiles, and tuataras, or they can become hard and calcified as in birds.

Jackson's Chameleon, Nairobi National Park, Kenya, *Chamaeleo jacksonii,* p.142
Life protects itself with scales and skin when it ventures inland. Reptilian scales provide armor, drought protection, and a means of communication. Hormones trigger color changes in pigment cells embedded in the scaly skin of a chameleon, enabling it to signal moods and intentions to others of its kind.

Thorny Devil, Central Australia, *Moloch horridus,* p. 143 (top)
The skin of a thorny devil, a small, ant-eating lizard that lives in the desert of central Australia, is covered in conical spikes and knobs, which serve as camouflage and defense against predatory reptiles. But it is the tiny channels that groove the surface of its skin that point to a remarkable adaptation to desert life. When a thorny devil walks through dewy vegetation or stands in a puddle, capillary action draws water up the channels in its skin until moisture gradually covers its body; when it finally spreads over its head, the thorny devil opens its mouth and water trickles in.

Blue-tongued Skink, Central Australia, *Tiliqua multifasciata,* p. 143 (bottom)
Skinks are lizards, but they move more like snakes. They have almost no neck, a long tapering tail, and very small limbs; some skinks get by with no legs at all. Their skin is covered in smooth scales that minimize resistance as they slither across sand.

Nile Crocodiles, Okavango Delta, Botswana, *Crocodylus niloticus,* pp. 144–145
Crocodiles are not dinosaurs, but they share a common ancestry. Both descended from archosaurs, or "ruling lizards," which arose 250 million years ago and radiated into the myriad reptilian species who dominated Earth for the next 185 million years. Some early archosaurs were low-slung, meat-eating quadrupeds with narrow skulls and long tails who looked a lot like crocodiles. One night in a swamp in northern Botswana when I witnessed dozens of crocodiles in action as they tore a dead hippo apart, it was not difficult to appreciate the power that large predatory dinosaurs once possessed.

Sand Dunes, Central Australia, pp. 146–147
But as continents move, climates change. Just as wind blows parallel sand dunes across Australia's central desert, this continent itself drifts slowly across the Earth, pushed by huge convection currents of magma beneath the surface. Throughout time continents have merged and collided and torn apart again. One day when I flew into the heart of Australia in a small plane, on a flight that lasted for hours, I had a chance to imagine the arid conditions on ancient Gondwana, which formed when the giant landmass of Pangaea broke apart into two supercontinents 200 million years ago. North of the Equator, Europe, Asia, and North America were joined as Laurasia, while to the south, Gondwana included what is now Africa, South America, Antarctica, Australia, New Zealand, India, and Madagascar.

Tree Fern Forest, Whirinaki Conservation Park, New Zealand, *Cyathea smithii,* p. 149
When I hiked into a tree fern forest on New Zealand's North Island, I felt like I was walking back in time. These tree ferns look just like their ancestors did around 320 million years ago, when much of the world was warm and tropical. But those ferns adapted to changing conditions when New Zealand moved to cooler latitudes after it separated from Gondwana, and now they form lush forests in a temperate maritime climate.

Redwoods in Fog, Monterey Bay, California, *Sequoia sempervirens,* pp. 150–151
I live next to a forest of giants. From my home on a meadow overlooking the Pacific Ocean I can see them towering over all other trees. They are redwoods, and they have a long history. In the days of dinosaurs they were widespread, but nowadays they only thrive in the narrow strip of California coast where hot land meets cold ocean. That is where fog forms which provides them with moisture during the summer months when there is no rain. One day when I hovered in a helicopter above a dense layer of fog moving inland, the tops of a grove of these giant trees emerged like ramparts in the sky.

Spruces in Snow, Finland, *Picea obovata,* pp. 152–153
Conifers adapt to cooling in times when Earth turns frigid. The movement of Earth's landmasses over time has contributed to the waxing and waning of polar ice caps, to periods of steamy warmth or glaciation, and even to extinction events that have punctuated the history of life on Earth. Spruces covered by deep snow during Finland's long winter show how well conifers can cope with cold, and to me they are a symbol of life's ability to respond to adversity with resilience.

INTO THE AIR

Greater Flamingos, Makgadikgadi Pans, Botswana, *Phoenicopterus ruber,* p. 154
In birds life gains new mobility. Flamingos cover continents. A flock of flamingos flies over water towards a large nesting colony that had just formed at the edge of an ephemeral lake. As I flew past them in a small plane, I wondered whether they had come from the coast of Namibia, 800 miles to the west, or from a distant lake in Africa's Great Rift Valley, 1,500 miles to the north. Either way, they would have reached this isolated lake in the middle of the Kalahari Desert only after a long journey across dry land without any water in between. How they knew that there was a suitable place to nest here, where there had been no water just months before, was a mystery to me, but the fact that they did it confirmed the miraculous ability of birds to commute between distant spots on the Earth like no other creatures can—on a moment's notice.

***Archaeopteryx* Fossil, Solnhofen, Germany,** *Archaeopteryx lithographica,* p. 156
One early form left an imprint like it fell only yesterday. A winged creature died in mud along the shoreline of a warm lagoon 150 million years ago, and was immortalized when it was found in a limestone quarry in southern Germany in 1860—just one year after the publication of Charles Darwin's book *On the Origin of Species.* Named *Archaeopteryx,* meaning "ancient wing," this exquisite fossil was immediately heralded as the missing link between dinosaurs and birds. Like birds, *Archaeopteryx* had feathered wings, but like reptiles, it had teeth, a long, bony tail, and claws on its wings. The discovery lent strong support to Darwin's revolutionary idea that species could change over time.

Magnificent Frigatebird, Galápagos Islands, *Fregata magnificens,* p. 157
Others fly today like visions from the past. A burst of light from my strobe etches the wing patterns of a frigatebird in twilight air as it hovers near my boat, drifting off one of the Galápagos's cactus-lined islands. The resulting image made me think of the imprint left in stone by *Archaeopteryx*. But there is another reason to link frigatebirds with flying reptiles: Their narrow, bent wings and soaring flight dynamics show parallels with pterosaurs, which took to the air long before birds evolved.

Laysan Albatross in Flight, French Frigate Shoals, Hawaiian Islands National Wildlife Refuge, Hawaii, *Diomedea immutabilis,* p. 158
Albatrosses at sea fly like hitchhikers on the wind. These legendary seabirds tap the wind's energy to conserve their own, covering phenomenal distances in ceaseless loops that take them across the world's oceans. Scientists have recently discovered that an albatross in flight spends barely more energy than one sitting down on the ground doing nothing.

Sooty Terns at Dusk, French Frigate Shoals, Hawaiian Islands National Wildlife Refuge, Hawaii, *Sterna fuscata,* pp. 160–161
Migrations get underway. Sooty terns fill the air at dusk as they approach their nests on an atoll in the central Pacific after a day of fishing offshore. As light fades away they become flying ghosts. All night long I heard their haunting calls above the pounding of surf on the reef. When young sooty terns fledge, they vanish into the open ocean for up to six years before they return to land again to reproduce.

Bird of Paradise Tail Feathers, California Academy of Sciences, San Francisco, California, *Paradisaea raggiana,* p. 162
Birds and feathers define each other: Every bird has feathers, and every creature that has feathers today is a bird. The basic design of feathers has remained virtually unchanged since they first appeared. A feather dropped by an *Archaeopteryx* could pass for one belonging to a modern bird. Feathers evolved from reptilian scales, but over time their specific forms have diversified to suit the needs of the more than 8,600 species of birds alive today. Feathers range from tiny down fuzz lining the bellies of hummingbirds to the outrageous plumes of peacocks. These specialized filamentous tail feathers of a male bird of paradise are used in courtship displays. They no longer insulate the bird against cold or water, nor do they provide lift for flight.

Western Gull Feather, Monterey Bay, California, *Larus occidentalis,* p. 163
Light shining through a western gull feather reveals its ingenious structure. From a central shaft, branches extend and divide into sub-branches linked together by hooklets, creating a solid surface that is airtight and waterproof, yet retains flexibility. Feathers are made of the same protein, keratin, as human fingernails. As a multifunctional, lightweight coat that insulates birds and carries them aloft, feathers are a remarkable innovation that enabled birds to become the most mobile creatures on Earth.

Black Heron Fishing, Okavango Delta, Botswana, *Egretta ardesiaca,* p. 164
Birds witness the emergence of flowering plants. The shape of a black heron fishing within the compound of its own cupped wings reminded me of the emerging blossom of a water lily growing in the same lagoon. The first birds and flowering plants evolved within ten million years of each other, and they've been entwined ever since.

Water Lily, Okavango Delta, Botswana, *Nymphaea nouchali,* p. 165
I sank waist-deep into a lagoon for an eye-level view of a water lily blossom spreading its petals, just as its ancestors have done for nearly 140 million years. Water lilies are among the oldest lineages of flowering plants. Prior to the evolution of flowers, most plants relied on wind to disperse their pollen. Flowering plants replaced that scattered approach with a targeted partnership between themselves and the animals who became their pollinators.

Giant Water Lily, Pantanal, Brazil, *Victoria regia*, p. 166
The corrugated leaf pad of a water lily serves as flotation device and solar panel, steadying the plant at the water's surface and providing a platform for photosynthesis.

***Pachypodium* Flower, Richtersveld National Park, South Africa,** *Pachypodium namaquanum*, p. 167
At first glance, the wrinkled appearance of the unfolding foliage of a *Pachypodium* may echo the corrugated structure of a lily pad, but these two plants could not be farther apart. One is a desert dweller from South Africa; the other, a swamp plant from Brazil. Yet what they have in common is a shared ancestry. Both are flowering plants, or angiosperms, which have blossomed into 235,000 species and now dominate Earth's vegetation from deserts to wetlands to forests.

Protea Flower, Kirstenbosch National Botanical Garden, Cape Town, South Africa, *Leucospermum cordifolium*, p. 168
Competition between flowering plants to attract pollinators triggered a proliferation of flower designs. The earliest protea flowers have their origin in Gondwana, around 90 million years ago. Since then, this family has radiated into more than 1,500 species of trees, shrubs, and herbs, many of them with extravagant flowers meant to lure specific pollinating partners.

Ant on *Euphorbia* Flower, Richtersveld National Park, South Africa, *Camponotus* sp. and *Euphorbia* sp., p. 169
Coevolution entwines insects and birds with plants forever. A black desert ant sips nectar from the tiny flowers of a *Euphorbia*. Insects had been around for more than 250 million years when flowering plants evolved, but flowers gave them new opportunities to expand, and within a few million years of the first flowers they began to diversify as ants, bees, butterflies, and many more new forms, developing ever more intricate partnerships with flowers. Today insects and flowering plants are the two most diverse groups of living organisms on Earth.

Malachite Sunbird and Protea Flower, South Africa, *Nectarinia famosa* and *Leucospermum reflexum*, p. 170
A male sunbird sticks his long tongue into the interior of a protea flower, seeking nectar. As he fumbles in the flower, pollen brushes onto his face. Many flowers evolved structures that oblige birds to struggle to get to their reward, forcing pollen into physical contact with the bird's plumage and increasing the chance that it is successfully carried to another flower of the same kind.

Green-crowned Brilliant Hummingbird Feeding on Ginger Flower, Monteverde Cloud Forest Reserve, Costa Rica, *Heliodoxa jacula* and *Costus montanus*, p. 171
I knew that hummingbirds would not be able to resist this luscious ginger flower at the edge of a cloud forest, so I set up my camera and waited; it wasn't long before a green-crowned brilliant buzzed in and sucked nectar while hovering in front of the flower, unaffected by bursts of light from my three strobes. Hummingbirds are an extreme consequence of a sugar-fueled existence. They are totally dependent on nectar to maintain their high-energy lifestyle, and zip from flower to flower with wing beats of up to 80 per second. From a plant's perspective, hummingbirds are ideal pollinators: They are small and fast, and they need to visit many flowers in a short amount of time to get enough food--a perfect recipe for successful flower pollination.

Kakapo, Codfish Island, New Zealand, *Strigops habroptilus*, p. 172
When birds can't fly they become vulnerable. When New Zealand broke away as a sliver of Gondwana around 80 million years ago, it became an evolutionary raft of birds. Land mammals never made it to New Zealand, and that absence of predatory pressure allowed birds to evolve in wondrous ways. A parrot with noisy Australian ancestors turned into a flightless vegetarian that roams the forest after dark in search of seeds. Kakapos are the heaviest parrots in the world. They are very rare today and most of them now live on only one island off New Zealand, where invading rats and stoats can't get to them. One memorable rainy evening I caught up with a kakapo. Actually it caught up with me. A curious female came to check me out as I was lying flat on my stomach on the muddy forest floor, camera in one hand, strobe in the other.

Brown Kiwi, New Zealand, *Apteryx australis,* p. 173

New Zealand's flightless kiwis are avian anomalies; in some ways they are more like mammals than birds. They have catlike whiskers on their faces, heavy marrow-filled bones, and hairy plumage that feels like fur. And as I found out one night when I joined a researcher who retrieved one from a burrow, they have the pungent odor of a peccary. The only birds with external nostrils at the tips of their beaks, kiwis use their acute sense of smell to find earthworms after dark, filling the niche of shrews and moles who specialize in hunting worms in other parts of the world. It is believed that kiwis evolved from larger, ostrich-size ancestors which grew smaller in New Zealand's forests. But their eggs didn't shrink nearly as much as the birds themselves, and female kiwis now have the unenviable task of laying the world's largest eggs relative to body size. A kiwi egg can weigh one-fourth as much as the mother herself.

Silversword at Sunset, Mauna Kea, Hawaii, *Argyroxiphium sandwicense,* p. 174

In Hawaii a daisy becomes a silversword. I had to climb into thin air to find the spectacular silverswords that grow on the upper slopes of Hawaii's volcanoes. They are the dramatically modified descendants of tiny daisies from California, which were carried across thousands of miles of open ocean to Hawaii as stowaway seeds caught in the plumage of birds. In Hawaii these daisy seeds took root and eventually evolved into more than two dozen new species of silverswords.

Octopus Trees, Southern Madagascar, *Didierea trollii,* pp. 176–177

The spiny desert of southern Madagascar is as otherworldly as any place I've ever visited. Ninety-five percent of all plants that grow here live nowhere else on Earth. Among the most striking sights in this arid bush are the twisted tentacles of the octopus tree, which looks like a cactus but is not. Its resemblance to a cactus is an example of convergent evolution, the process by which unrelated life-forms in different locations evolve the same appearance when subjected to similar conditions. In order to get this view of interlacing branches I had to work myself gingerly into the midst of an octopus tree thicket, and I soon learned how effective the structural defense of this plant is against animals: I had to ask for help to get myself untangled.

Aloe in Bloom, Southern Madagascar, *Aloe vaombe,* p. 178

All plants store water, but succulents survive in arid environments by storing large amounts for long periods of time in fleshy leaves and stems covered with a waterproof waxy skin. I kneeled below this plant to silhouette it against the intense glow of a sunset caused by dust from a volcanic eruption 5,000 miles away.

King Protea, Kirstenbosch National Botanical Garden, Cape Town, South Africa, *Protea cynaroides,* p. 179

In ancient Gondwana, drought molds proteas. This king protea whose blossoms are opening at the base of Cape Town's Table Mountain is the most spectacular of all the proteas. The origin of this plant family is in Gondwana, where drying conditions shaped their appearance and their habits. Proteas developed leathery leaves that help them resist desiccation during the hot, dry summers, along with other adaptations for surviving periodic wildfires, including thick bark and fireproof cones to protect their seeds.

Palo Santo Trees, Galápagos Islands, *Bursera graveolens,* pp. 180–181

Even though they live near the Equator, palo santo trees in the Galápagos are deciduous—like many trees in temperate climates—but instead of dropping their leaves when it's cold, they shed them when it's hot, to minimize water loss. When it rains the trees come back to life, as they are doing in this image made after an El Niño winter had unleashed torrential rains on the islands.

Baobabs in Winter, Western Madagascar, *Adansonia grandidieri,* p. 182

With their majestic size and distinctive shape, baobabs stand out in every landscape where they occur. Like most of the trees that surround them, they are flowering plants. Baobabs are icons of African lore, but it is the island of Madagascar that nurtures the most species—six versus Africa's one. Like succulents, baobabs can store a lot of water in their thick, fibrous trunks. But they become leafless in winter when it is dry on Madagascar's coastal plain.

Grass Trees in Wind, Western Australia, *Xanthorrhoea preissii*, p. 183
In Australia a lily turns into a grass tree. In the arid bushlands of Western Australia, an area prone to wildfires, an ordinary lily was molded over time into an extraordinary tree with a grassy crown whose thick trunk shelters the plant from the fires that would otherwise kill it. As it evolved, the grass tree's relationship with fire has become more complex: Fire now triggers the emergence of its flowering stalks, which extend ten feet high or more.

Buttressed Trees, Cockscomb Basin Wildlife Sanctuary, Belize, pp. 184–185
Jungles arise, sparking new layers of interdependence. After Gondwana began to break apart around 100 million years ago, life got lush. In tropical latitudes new winds began to blow moisture-laden air from warm seas inland, where humid forests took root in which flowering plants multiplied rapidly in shape and size, eventually growing into the bewildering jungles that we know as tropical rainforests today.

Bracket Fungi on Logs, Congo Basin, Democratic Republic of Congo Basin, p. 186
Fungi multiply. Where plants thrive, so do fungi. They are invisible partners of plants and essential recyclers of nutrients in the web of life. Fungi live underground or inside other organisms. Their lifestyle may seem alien, yet on the tree of life fungi sit in between plants and animals, sharing characteristics of both.

Cup Fungi, Mount Kinabalu National Park, Borneo, *Cookeina tricholoma*, p. 187
What may look like flowers at first glance are actually the fruiting bodies of a fungus growing inside a decaying log in a rainforest in Borneo.

Stapelia Flower, Richtersveld National Park, South Africa, *Orbea namaquensis*, p. 188
An unassuming succulent plant, growing mere inches off the ground in a South African desert, erupts into bloom with a flower that mimics the smell of rotting flesh. The odor is meant to attract carrion flies, their preferred pollinators. It's the scent that brings in the flies, but the patterns on the flower reinforce recognition.

Orchid, Native to Peru, Private Collection, *Oncidium hastilabium*, p. 189
Orchids comprise the single largest family of flowering plants, with close to 30,000 species. Their spectacular diversity is supported by intricate partnerships with pollinators and fungi. In the wild, each orchid appears to have unique associations with certain species of root fungi. This kind of symbiosis has a downside: Once an orchid becomes dependent on a specific pollinator and a fungal partner, its survival is linked with theirs.

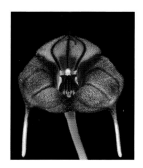

Orchid, Native to Peru, Private Collection, *Masdevallia* sp., p. 190
Orchids emerge, their genitalia shaped to lure insects. Runway guides and landing spots lure insects into the center of an orchid native to the cloud forests of the Andes. This pink specimen is a cultivated hybrid nurtured to please human eyes, but in the wild an orchid's appearance depends on the preference of its pollinators, which include bees, flies, spiders, birds, bats, moths, and other animals. Orchids have evolved complex strategies for making sure that pollinators actually carry away pollen. One orchid fires a tiny pollen-tipped dart when a bee lands on its lip, and another one attracts male wasps with a scent that mimics the irresistible pheromone of a female wasp.

Orchid, Native to Peru, Private Collection, *Masdevallia* sp., p. 191
By focusing in closely on the heart of an orchid illuminated from behind, I tried to create a sensation of flying into the center of this flower, which is designed to lure insects, not with fragrance or nectar, but with color and shape.

Wildfire, Los Padres National Forest, Big Sur, California, pp. 192–193
When an asteroid hits the Earth, a world vanishes in flames. An asteroid six miles in diameter hit Earth 65 million years ago near Mexico's Yucatán Peninsula. The shock wave of the impact emptied the entire Gulf of Mexico, causing cataclysmic tsunamis to rush across North America. The amount of molten rock thrown into the air by the impact has been estimated at the size of a small European country dug up to a depth of five miles. The hot debris soon fell back down to Earth and started massive wildfires all across the Northern Hemisphere. Clouds of dust and smoke blanketed the planet, smothering life. Standing at the advancing edge of a wildfire raging through a dry forest along the coast of California gave me a physical sense of the extinguishing force of fire.

Redwoods in Evening Fog, Monterey Bay, California, *Sequoia sempervirens,* pp. 194–195
But there are witnesses, survivors in the dark. In the months that followed the asteroid impact, light faded from the sky. It became dark, and life came to a standstill. Within a few years, more than half of all life-forms on Earth died out. No large land animals survived. All large dinosaurs went extinct. In the oceans nearly all plankton, which depend on sunlight for photosynthesis, expired. Some scientists believe that massive volcanic outbreaks during this same era contributed to the extinctions that occurred, but few doubt the significance of the asteroid event as an evolutionary shake-up. Among the survivors of this holocaust, known as the Cretaceous-Tertiary, or K-T, Extinction, were redwoods, like these shrouded by dense evening fog.

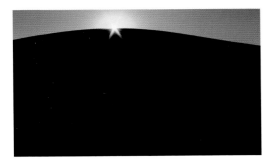

Sunrise over Hillside, California, pp. 196–197
When the skies clear, a new world is born . . . Times of crisis are times of opportunity: Among the life-forms that survived the extinction bottleneck were birds and early mammals, and they inherited a world empty of giant beasts.

OUT OF THE DARK

Elephant and Greater Kudu at Dawn, Chobe National Park, Botswana, *Loxodonta africana* and *Tragelaphus strepsiceros*, p. 198
A world fit for mammals . . . The first mammals evolved from reptiles at least 210 million years ago, but during their initial 145 million years they lived in the shadows of dinosaurs. Those early mammals are not well known, but most of them were probably small, nocturnal creatures. It was the demise of dinosaurs that triggered a spectacular diversification of mammals into the more than 4,000 species alive today. At an African waterhole I waited for the moment when a kudu passed behind an elephant to frame both as examples of different mammalian forms.

Giant Hedgehog Skull, Naturalis, the National Museum of Natural History, Leiden, Netherlands,
Deinogalerix koenigswaldi, p. 200
Mammalian teeth are precision tools and they are shaped according to the habits of their users. In a Dutch museum I marveled at the teeth of a strange hedgehog, now extinct, that lived on an island off Italy in the Adriatic Sea six million years ago. It became a predator and grew into a giant hedgehog ten times the size of an ordinary one. Its long incisors resembling those of a fox or a cat were used to seize small mammals instead of the earthworms that today's humbler hedgehogs pursue as prey.

Large Treeshrew, Danum Valley Conservation Area, Borneo, *Tupaia tana,* p. 201
From tiny shrew-like creatures accustomed to the dark, new forms radiate. Treeshrews are squirrel-size mammals who bounce around like pinballs through the rainforests of Borneo, often moving so fast that I noticed little more than a rustle in the leaf litter. They are not true shrews, nor are they the primitive primates scientists once thought they were. But their furtive behavior and frenetic lifestyle gave me a sense of the lives of the early mammals they resemble. When this resting treeshrew yawned, it revealed rows of tiny sharp teeth used for chewing on insects and fruits.

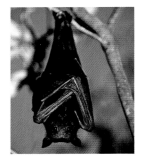

Little Red Flying Fox, Daintree National Park, Queensland, Australia, *Pteropus scapulatus,* p. 202
I could hear them before I saw them. A cacophony of shrill, squeaky voices led me to a gathering of little red flying foxes in a daytime roost, where they dangled upside down from mangrove trees. They didn't fly until it got dark, for fear of getting grabbed in mid-flight by the eagles that patrolled overhead. At twilight I photographed one flying fox waking up and staring down at me, just before it vanished into the night sky to search for blossoms in eucalyptus groves. While flying foxes use sight and scent to find food, other bats echolocate, emitting sounds that bounce back to their ears, creating a sonic image of their prey on which they zero in. Some fossils of early bats preserve delicate ear bones which reveal that 49 million years ago they were already equipped to echolocate.

Malayan Civet, Danum Valley Conservation Area, Borneo, *Viverra tangalunga,* p. 203
Civets are catlike in size and shape and make a living as fruit-eaters and ambush hunters after dark. This young civet peering from the base of a buttressed tree in a rainforest on Borneo made me think of a time when the decline of predatory reptiles gave mammals a chance to move out and assume new identities as omnivores and carnivores.

Spotted Hyena, Okavango Delta, Botswana, *Crocuta crocuta,* p. 204
Running towards a lion kill at dusk, a spotted hyena displays the loping gait and opportunistic attitude that is characteristic of these unusual carnivores. In the course of many nocturnal encounters with them, I have come to appreciate hyenas as formidable predators in their own right, who can hold their own against lions. Often it is the lions who are scavengers around hyena kills, rather than the other way around. Hyenas may look part-dog, part-cat, and part-bear, but the four living species belong to a lineage of their own. Strong jaw muscles and massive teeth enable spotted hyenas to break the bones of prey with crushing force in order to consume both the calcium-rich bones and the nutritious marrow inside.

Maned Wolf, Pantanal, Brazil, *Chrysocyon brachyurus,* p. 205
Wolves stalk on stilt legs in Brazil. Not all wolves are long-distance runners who live in packs. The shaggy-haired maned wolf is a solitary hunter whose long legs are adapted to the tall grass savannas of South America, where it prowls and pounces on small rodents which it detects with large ultrasensitive ears.

Giant Anteater, Pantanal, Brazil, *Myrmecophaga tridactyla,* p. 207
There are many ways to be a mammal. Giant anteaters see poorly, but they hear well and their sense of smell is excellent. Knowing that, I was able to follow one on foot by keeping quiet and staying downwind. I crouched low to the ground when this strangely shaped and patterned creature walked past me. Giant anteaters are toothless. They live on a diet of pure ants and termites, which they lick up with long, sticky tongues from cuts at the base of anthills sliced open with their powerful claws. A thick coat of long hair protects them from the stinging bites of soldier ants and termites, and helps to maintain their body temperature, which can fluctuate down to 89.6 degrees, the lowest of any terrestrial mammal. Forty-nine million years ago, anteaters lived in what is now Europe, but these days they are restricted to the warm parts of South America.

California Sea Lions, Monterey Bay, California, *Zalophus californianus,* pp. 208–209
Some mammals turn back to water; sea lions get sleek and adapt to cold with layers of fat. By crawling around on all fours on a beach packed with barking sea lions not far from my home in coastal California, I was able to keep a low profile so I wouldn't be detected as an upright primate. Shuffling around awkwardly on knees and elbows gave me an appreciation of how it must feel for sea lions to move around on land when they're really made to swim in the sea. The forelimbs of sea lions have become paddles, a feature reflected in the name of the taxonomic family to which they belong, pinnipeds, which means "finned feet." Their barks hark back to doglike ancestors, carnivores who began to adapt to a marine environment around 20 million years ago.

Spinner Dolphin, Midway Island, Midway Atoll National Wildlife Refuge, Hawaii, *Sternella longirostris,* p. 210
Whales and dolphins move into a world without bounds. One day when I joined a researcher on a turquoise lagoon for a marine survey in a small open boat, a curious spinner dolphin came to check us out. As we moved along, the dolphin kept crisscrossing our bow, apparently enjoying the encounter as much as we did. While hanging over the bow of the boat, I brought my camera close to the dolphin to create a wide-angle view of a creature at home in the boundless space of the open ocean. Like bats using sonar in the night sky, dolphins use echolocation to "see" with sound underwater. Making high-pitched squeaks and ultrasonic clicks that rebound off objects back to their ears, dolphins navigate by interpreting the echoes.

Beluga, Vancouver Aquarium, Canada, *Delphinapterus leucas,* p. 211
Around 50 million years ago a long-bodied land mammal with hoofed feet that looked a bit like a giant otter began a remarkable transformation. In a matter of a few million years it turned into a marine creature with webbed feet that resembled a seal, with eyes high on its head and limbs that were turning into flippers. Another few million years later it had evolved a massively muscled tail that propelled it through the water, and by 35 million years ago its hind limbs had disappeared. But deep inside the bodies of whales today, tiny bones of vestigial rear legs are reminders of their former identity.

Eastern Gray Kangaroo, Murramarang National Park, Australia, *Macropus giganteus,* p. 212
Kangaroos hop in Australia. By lying flat on the ground and aiming a long lens at a bounding kangaroo while a friend pointed a strobe at it from the side, I was able to freeze an impression of its unique pattern of locomotion. It has been suggested that the hopping of kangaroos on two legs is more energy efficient than running on four legs. As a kangaroo leaps, the energy of its bound is recaptured in the tendons of its legs when it lands, and that energy propels the next leap, like a pogo stick. The big tail of this eastern gray kangaroo serves as a counterbalance during its leaps, and also stores fat for lean times.

Takhi, Hustain Nuruu National Park, Mongolia, *Equus przewalskii,* p. 213
Horses run in Asia. The fabled Przewalski's horse, or takhi, as it is called in its homeland of Mongolia, is the only true wild horse left in the world today. All other horses are either domesticated animals or their feral descendants. Pleistocene cave art in Europe reveals that wild horses similar to takhi were once common there. But as climates changed and humans and their livestock spread, takhi dwindled in Europe and Asia, and eventually they became extinct in the wild. From a handful of individual takhi lingering in zoos, a captive breeding program led to their successful reintroduction into the wilds of Mongolia. That is where I created this image of a takhi in motion. By using a slow shutter speed and panning along as it ran past me, I was able to highlight the vitality of an animal wild once more. But to me this image also echoes the immortal paintings of the takhi's Ice Age relatives made on cave walls in France by anonymous artists 30,000 years ago.

Burchell's Zebras, Masai Mara National Reserve, Kenya, *Equus burchelli,* pp. 214–215
Grasslands create opportunities . . . This image of three zebras grazing on the fertile grasslands of eastern Africa is a simplified expression of the intricate coevolution that connects grasses and grazers. When global climates began to get cooler and drier starting around 35 million years ago, forests gave way to more open habitats worldwide. Prairies arose in North America, steppes in Eurasia, pampas in South America, and savannas in Africa. Grasses spread and grazing mammals proliferated. In response to grazing pressure, grasses formed more abrasive silica crystals inside their leaves. That in turn resulted in grazers developing higher-crowned teeth hard enough for a lifetime of consuming coarse grass.

Impalas, Okavango Delta, Botswana, *Aepyceros melampus,* pp. 216–217
. . . where safety comes from sharpened senses. I had to climb onto the roof of my Land Rover to see this herd of impalas moving into the shelter of tall summer grasses, where eyes and ears serve as a common defense for these social antelopes.

Cheetah, Namibia, *Acinonyx jubatus,* p. 218
Getting faster . . . The open spaces of grasslands triggered new forms of predators and prey. From ancestral cats built for stalking and ambushing, cheetahs evolved into sleek specialists and became the world's fastest animals on four legs. A cheetah's body is geared for its explosive sprint. An ultra-flexible spine helps extend its powerful, long-legged strides, and the cheetah's extra-long tail serves as an essential counterbalance as it adjusts to the swerving of its prey. I've witnessed cheetahs accelerate to speeds of 60 miles an hour—but I've also seen how a 20-second sprint exhausted a cheetah so completely that it had to rest for half an hour before it could begin to feed on the gazelle it had brought down.

Impala, Masai Mara National Reserve, Kenya, *Aepyceros melampus,* p. 219
. . . and faster still. A leaping impala to me is an embodiment of grace in motion. Its body is shaped by pressures imposed on it by predators like cheetahs. Ever longer and lighter leg bones have kept impalas one leap ahead of their enemies over time.

Elephant and Impala, Chobe National Park, Botswana, *Loxodonta africana* and *Aepyceros melampus*, p. 220
Growing big is another answer, but size often comes at a price. Elephants are among the last of the great mega-herbivores that once roamed Earth on all continents except Antarctica. Changes in climate, resources, and the impact of humans have since favored smaller herbivores like antelopes. I wanted to contrast the archaic shape of an elephant and the modern form of an impala as both drank from the same waterhole. I positioned myself so that the elephant was in the foreground and then used a long lens to compress the distance between both animals, which had the optical effect of making the elephant even larger relative to the impala than it already was.

Elephants, Impalas, and Doves, Chobe National Park, Botswana,
Loxodonta africana, Aepyceros melampus, and *Streptopelia capicola*, pp. 222–223
The mega-mammal world of the Pleistocene comes alive at a waterhole in the arid woodlands of northern Botswana, where a group of elephants towers above diminutive impalas and fluttering doves.

Lowland Rainforest, Danum Valley Conservation Area, Borneo, pp. 224–225
Primates evolve in jungles. Tropical forests were the ecological wombs in which primates developed bodies and senses adapted to treetop living. Grasping limbs and fluid locomotion became imperative for survival. Stereoscopic vision superseded smell as a way to make sense of hazards and opportunities, and in time primates developed superb color vision. A tropical forest photographed at dawn hints at the world that nurtured early primates.

Tarsier, Sabah, Borneo, *Tarsius bancanus*, p. 226
Tarsiers first . . . Tarsiers have been called dawn monkeys; they are believed to be living links to a branch of early primates who evolved in the rainforests of Southeast Asia some 50 million years ago. Tarsiers use their huge eyes to hunt for insects in the dark understory of the Borneo night. Like all primates, they do not possess reflective structures in the backs of their eyes, which boost night vision for other nocturnal creatures such as cats. To make up for this deficiency, tarsiers evolved the largest eyes of any living primate. The size of a tarsier's eyeball equals the size of its brain.

Sifaka, Berenty Reserve, Madagascar, *Propithecus verreauxi*, p. 227
. . . lemurs not much later. In a dry forest in Madagascar I came eye-to-eye with the languid stare of a sifaka resting in a tree fork on a hot summer day. Lemurs represent a separate lineage of early primates who once lived throughout Europe and North America when climates were warmer around 50 million years ago; they vanished there when climates changed. In Africa lemurs were outcompeted by later-evolving monkeys, but in the isolation of Madagascar's island universe where monkeys never occurred, lemurs survived. They underwent their own radiation into dozens of different species that range from a tiny mouse lemur the size of a fist to indris that resemble young pandas.

Female Bonobo and Infant, Native to the Congo Basin, *Pan paniscus*, p. 229
Bands of apes venture into the open when forests dry out once more. Somewhere in the heart of Africa perhaps around five million years ago, a few groups of forest-dwelling apes began to exploit new opportunities on the ground when climate change shrank forests, and open woodland and savannas expanded again. Sometime during that transition, knuckle-walking apes began to adopt an upright posture. Bonobos today spend most of their time in trees, and when they come down to the ground they tend to walk on all fours, such as this female does in a captive colony. But at times I have seen them walk upright, providing a haunting glimpse back in time.

Chimpanzee Male, Kenya, *Pan troglodytes*, p. 230
So who are we? Brothers of masculine chimps? Observations of wild apes in combination with studies of captive individuals have made it clear how fuzzy the boundaries between ourselves and our next of kin really are. Interestingly, the characters of our two nearest living relatives embody two different aspects of human nature. Chimps live in societies dominated by males who are fiercely competitive and often aggressive. They wage war and kill their own. Even in encounters with captive individual chimps, such as this young male, I have learned to be on guard.

Bonobo Female, Native to the Congo Basin, *Pan paniscus,* p. 231
Sisters of feminine bonobos? Bonobos were formerly called pygmy chimpanzees. These gracile apes live only in the dark forests of the central Congo Basin and were long ignored by researchers and conservationists. Their character reflects a different kind of society. Cooperation between females, rather than competition between males, is at the heart of the bonobo's lifestyle. Females dominate males and social tensions are often resolved through sexual interactions. This female is one of only a few dozen bonobos in captivity. The fate of the wild population hangs in the balance due to ongoing civil unrest in their homeland.

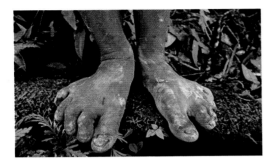

Ashaninka Indian Feet, Vilcabamba, Peru, *Homo sapiens,* pp. 232–233
Going upright becomes a lifestyle. On an expedition in the upper Amazon Basin of Peru, I was amazed by the bare feet of an Ashaninka Indian who guided me through a tropical forest. When we paused for a break I learned that he had never worn shoes in his life; in fact, he had never been out of the forest. I had been looking for an image that would symbolize how the bodies of humans are shaped by nature. This man's feet looked quite different from mine, and it made me realize how easily human limbs can change shape under the pressures of a natural environment. When my guide walked across a fallen log, I had a chance to photograph him. Gloomy light conditions in the forest necessitated fill flash, so I aimed a strobe with one hand while operating my camera with the other, tasks that only a primate with grasping hands and opposable thumbs could accomplish simultaneously.

Human Fetus, National Museum of Health and Medicine, Washington, D.C., *Homo sapiens,* p. 235
We are all of them and more. The bodies of all living organisms, including those of humans, carry within them the story of life itself, as it has evolved on Earth. Each individual feature connects us to a previous stage in evolution and to other life-forms who share them. Our most distinctive hominoid characteristic, a big brain, evolved less than five million years ago, and we have it in common with our next of kin, the great apes. We share hair with all other mammals, and internal fertilization with all birds and reptiles. We share four limbs with all amphibians, and an internal skeleton with all fishes. We share chromosomes and an aerobic metabolism with all plants, fungi, and protists, such as algae and diatoms. And within every one of our cells are structures that date back to the origin of all living organisms and that reveal the fundamental unity of all life, even at the molecular level. Our connection with bacteria is our DNA, which shapes the way we grow. I photographed this developing human embryo in a medical research collection as an homage to the wonder of all life. Soft light coming through a window illuminated the delicate curves of its face and hands.

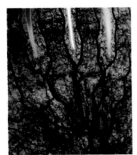

Blood Veins in Human Hand, Museum Boerhaave, Leiden, Netherlands, *Homo sapiens,* p. 236
The blood veins in our hands echo the course water traces on the Earth. A wafer-thin cross section through a human hand, prepared as a specimen for a medical teaching collection, reveals the intricate network of blood veins through which nutrients are circulated to all parts of the human body.

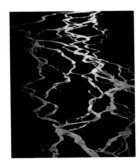

Braiding River, Wrangell-St. Elias National Park, Alaska, p. 237
Patterns within reflect patterns without: River drainages on the surface of the Earth distribute essential nutrients, just as blood vessels do within a human body, and serve as conduits through which water cycles endlessly between land, sea, and air.

PLANET OF LIFE

Rainforest and Granite Mountains, Serra dos Órgãos National Park, Brazil, p. 238
Life is a force in its own right. Looking at a tropical rainforest through a telephoto lens, I compressed its bewildering variety of life into overlapping layers of green covering granite outcrops to express the connections between life and Earth. The notion of life as a force that interacts with Earth and its atmosphere was articulated in the 1970s by scientist James Lovelock in his Gaia theory. Lovelock had been asked by NASA to devise instruments that could be sent to Mars on a spacecraft to detect whether life existed there. This led him to ponder the nature of life on Earth. He concluded that life's collective biochemical activities had made a crucial difference in establishing conditions on Earth that were conducive to the survival of life itself.

Volcanic Caldera, White Island, New Zealand, p. 240
It is a new element. From the rim of a volcano smoldering with fumes containing carbon dioxide and other gases, I stared into a landscape where life had yet to take hold. Before life emerged, large parts of the Earth may have looked like this barren caldera, shaped by geologic forces alone. It could have stayed that way, but on this planet things turned out differently.

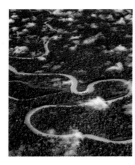

Meandering River, Manu National Park, Peru, p. 241
It has altered the Earth. After crossing the thin air and arid slopes of the Andes in a small plane one day, I descended into the steamy lowlands of the Amazon Basin where the glory of life on Earth unfolded in front of me, with morning clouds drifting above a river meandering through unbroken tropical forest extending to the horizon. So prevalent has life become on Earth after four billion years that in a philosophical sense, it can be regarded as a sixth element, joining the classic elements of earth, air, fire, water, and space originally recognized by ancient thinkers more than two thousand years ago.

Summer over Greenland, p. 242
The cosmic event that created the Moon from a collision between Earth and a proto-planet 4.5 billion years ago tilted the Earth on its axis. This has given life on Earth a seasonal pulse. It takes summer warmth for life to expand in Greenland. Melting snow and ice expose mountains patched with lichens and mosses, whose adaptations to harsh environments were shaped in an earlier age.

Winter over Greenland, pp. 244–245
In Greenland in winter, the margins for life become clear. When winter comes to Greenland, water solidifies as ice and life goes dormant. Without liquid water, photosynthesis in living cells comes to a halt and food chains collapse. The extremes of winter in the polar regions are one measure of the outer limits for life on Earth. I made this image of a lifeless landscape from a jetliner flying across Greenland on an early afternoon in December when the sun had already set.

Tundra Autumn, Wrangell-St. Elias National Park, Alaska, pp. 246–247
Life covers Earth like a skin. A thin veneer of tundra vegetation with glowing yellow bands of dwarf willow stretches across the rocky slope of a mountain in Alaska.

Fall Colors, Wrangell-St. Elias National Park, Alaska, pp. 248–249
Fall colors burst forth when deciduous plants quit producing chlorophyll as days grow shorter and cooler. The yellows and reds we see are stages in this seasonal retreat of life. In the Arctic the height of fall color comes and goes in a matter of days. I captured the fleeting nature of this phenomenon by contrasting the peaking colors on the slope in the foreground with those already fading on the opposite side.

Glacial Valley, Wrangell-St. Elias National Park, Alaska, pp. 250–251
A few degrees of temperature change can make the difference between a landscape covered by ice and one filled with trees. An advancing forest of pioneering conifers covers a valley floor scoured by a retreating glacier not long ago. Over time, changing climates have triggered periods of glaciation which in turn have reworked the surface of the Earth on every continent, grinding rocks into soil and releasing nutrients that fuel food chains.

Coastline, Big Sur, California, pp. 252–253
On a hike along the ridges of Big Sur, I came across limestone deposits left far above sea level by a retreating ocean. They contained fossilized marine shells made of carbonates. The movement of carbon through land, sea, air, and living organisms links Earth and life in an essential cycle. Volcanoes emit carbon dioxide which is absorbed by plants and oceans. It is also removed from the atmosphere through the weathering of rocks in a geochemical process that yields carbonates, which wash into the sea where they are taken up by marine organisms to make shells. When these creatures die, their shells settle on the seafloor and accumulate into limestone sediments. Over time this limestone sinks deeper into the Earth and eventually, some of its carbon dioxide is expelled again into the atmosphere by volcanoes, completing the cycle. One winter day, after overnight rain had drenched the Big Sur coast, sunlight and morning clouds blended land, sea, and air together, enabling me to capture this landscape as a dynamic visualization of a living Earth.

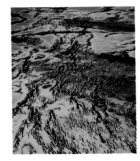

Seagrass Meadows, Shark Bay, Western Australia, *Zostera* sp., p. 254
But where water is liquid, it is a womb for cells green with chlorophyll. And that molecular marvel has made the difference. It fuels everything on Earth. From a small plane circling Shark Bay I could see strands of seagrasses shimmer in underwater meadows. They are marine flowering plants that grow in profusion in this warm bay, not far from the isolated inner lagoon which separates ancient stromatolites built by cyanobacteria from modern marine life. Almost everywhere on Earth, flowering plants along with marine algae have taken over from cyanobacteria as the major producers of oxygen today.

Coral Reefs, Great Barrier Reef, Australia, p. 255
The animal world today lives on oxygen released by algae, bacteria, and plants. Coral reefs pattern a shallow lagoon in Australia's Great Barrier Reef, the largest animal-made structure on Earth. Built by polyps that secrete calcium carbonate, coral reefs can be viewed as the successors of the stromatolite mounds made by cyanobacteria. The basis for the productivity of coral reefs is the algae that supply nutrients to the coral polyps, which shelter the algae in their tissues. The resulting coexistence is a grand expression of life as a symbiosis.

Surf, Bull Kelp, and Snares Crested Penguins, The Snares, New Zealand, *Durvillaea* sp. *and Eudyptes robustus,* pp. 256–257
I visualized the surging motion of an incoming tide with a time exposure as a wave swept through kelp along the shore of a forlorn island south of New Zealand. Millions of petrels and penguins use this island as a home base for a life that is dependent on the bounty of the surrounding sub-Antarctic waters.

Iguazú Falls, Iguazú National Park, Argentina, pp. 258–259
Earth's lifeblood is water. It evaporates from oceans and drifts over land as clouds. Rain falls, nurturing terrestrial life. Waters then collect into rivers that flow back into the sea, completing one of Earth's most fundamental cycles.

Morning Mist over Rainforest, Danum Valley Conservation Area, Borneo, pp. 260–261
This Earth is alive, and it has made its own membrane. A biosphere made of land, sea, and air, energized by all living things . . .
After spending weeks inside a tropical forest documenting the intricate details of its natural history, I took a helicopter ride one morning. As soon as I rose above the canopy, my view expanded to the forest as a whole. I saw morning mist wafting through the treetops and envisioned the collective exhalation of this forest as the breath of a living planet.

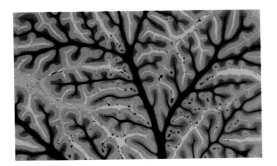

Monsoon Clouds over Indian Ocean, pp. 262–263
. . . forming a whole that is held together and sustained by the collective power of life. Only within the past generation have humans pierced the outer layers of the planetary membrane we call biosphere. A few have ventured into outer space, and unmanned probes have landed on distant planets, but perhaps the most important result of our explorations of other worlds has been to make us realize the uniqueness of our own. Viewed from space, Earth appears as an entity enveloped in swirls of clouds, visible evidence of the planet's atmospheric membrane. Few humans have been privileged to see Earth this way with their own eyes, but millions have gazed down on continents, oceans, and clouds from jet planes that crisscross the upper reaches of the biosphere every day. One day when I traveled across the Indian Ocean from Africa to Madagascar, I watched layers of monsoon clouds cast shadows on its sea. Sunlight diffracting through the plane's window created the semblance of a rainbow that underscored to me the ephemeral beauty of life on our water planet.

Human Brain, National Museum of Health and Medicine, Washington, D.C., *Homo sapiens,* p. 304
Our brains, our celebrated brains . . . enable us to imagine a whole Earth. What looks at first glance like the branching patterns in a tree or the flowing shapes of creeks in a coastal marsh are actually the patterns of a human cerebellum, an ancient part of the human brain which we have in common with all other vertebrates. I photographed this thin cross section of a human brain in a medical research collection. As humans we share up to 98 percent of our genes with our nearest relatives, chimpanzees and bonobos. It is the remaining two percent that makes us different, and enables us to understand and connect with all other expressions of life on Earth.

TIMELINE

For this journey from the past to the present I found it useful to have a timeline as a guide. I compiled a chronology of major Earth events from scientists and other authoritative sources with dates for the earliest known origins of the plants, animals, and other life-forms I came to know and appreciate in the course of this project. These dates are approximations, and many of them are at the center of active scientific debate and ongoing study. All of them are subject to change based on new findings or other interpretations. A selection of websites listed under "Timelines" in the "Resources" section provides more information.

There are many ways to journey through time. The itinerary of images and stories I made for this book is very personal. I chose the subjects because they resonated with me, and I offer them up as part of a larger view of life on Earth.

Event	Billions of years ago
Birth of the Universe	13.7
Birth of the Solar System and Earth	4.56
Moon Forms	4.5
Earth's Surface Solidifies	4.4
Early Atmosphere Forms	4.4
Earth Cools, Oceans Form	4.4–4.2
First Life	4.0–3.8
First Cyanobacteria	3.8–2.7
Banded Iron Deposits	3.8–2.4 and 1.9–1.8
Large Landmasses Form	3.0–2.5
First Eukaryotes	2.7
Oxygenated Atmosphere Forms	2.4
First Algae	1.8–1.2

	Millions of years ago
Ediacaran Period	**635–543**
Jellies	580
Corals	550
Cambrian Explosion	**543–510**
Mollusks	540
Arthropods	535
Trilobites	525
Echinoderms	525
Crinoids	505
Fungi	500
Eurypterids	480
Land Plants	470
Jawed Fishes	425
Spiders	420
Club Mosses	415
Lichens	400
Scorpions	400
Ammonoids	400
Insects	400
Horseshoe Crabs	400

Event	Millions of years ago
Giant Club Mosses	380
First Trees	380
Amphibians	370
Ferns	370
First Seed Plants	370
Mosses	370
Horsetails	370
Tree Ferns	320
Conifers	315
Land Snails	310
Reptiles and Amniotic Eggs	310
Pangaea	**290–200**
Cycads	280
Permian Extinction	**250**
Archosaurs	250
Tuataras	240
Dinosaurs	230
Crocodiles	230
Turtles	230
Araucarias	230
Pterosaurs	215
First Mammals	210
Diatoms	200
Tortoises	200
Redwoods	175
Gondwana Breaks Up	**160–30**
Birds	150
Flowering Plants	140
Water Lilies	140
Ants	130
Orchids	100
Proteas	90
Treeshrews	87
Cretaceous-Tertiary Extinction	**65**
Bats	57
Tarsiers	55
Horses	55
Lemurs	54
Whales	50
Elephants	50
Anteaters	49
Grasslands	35
Kangaroos	30
Albatrosses	30
Sea Lions	20
Hyenas	20
Antelopes	9
Giant Hedgehogs	6
Maned Wolves	3
Cheetahs	3
Chimpanzees	2.5
Bonobos	2.5
First Humans	2.5
Modern Humans	0.2

RESOURCES

Anyone can experience the journey of life through time. The web links listed below offer access to up-to-date information about the story of life on Earth. These links include some of the leading scientific and educational institutions engaged in research and outreach, the media and conservation organizations whose efforts dovetail with scientific discoveries, and a selection of the many outstanding museums and research collections where you can learn more about the subjects featured in this book. Other links are included for photographic resources and technical support.

SCIENCE AND EDUCATION

Scientific Institutions and Organizations:
American Association for the Advancement of Science, Washington, DC: www.aaas.org
Astrobiology at NASA: http://astrobiology.arc.nasa.gov
Earth System Science Center, University Park, PA: www.essc.psu.edu
Earth System Science Education, Columbia, MD: www.usra.edu/esse
European Space Agency, Paris, France: www.esa.int
National Aeronautics and Space Administration, Washington, DC: www.nasa.gov
NASA-Ames Research Center, Moffett Field, South San Francisco, CA: www.nasa.gov/
    centers/ames/home/index.html
National Academy of Sciences, Washington, DC: www.nas.edu
National Human Genome Research Institute, Bethesda, MD: www.genome.gov
National Science Foundation, Arlington, VA: www.nsf.gov
The Royal Society, London, England: www.royalsoc.ac.uk
Society for the Study of Evolution: www.evolutionsociety.org
United States Geological Survey, Washington, DC: www.usgs.gov
University of California Santa Cruz, Center for Biomolecular Science and Engineering:
    www.cbse.ucsc.edu

Education and Media:
British Broadcasting Corporation: www.bbc.co.uk
E. O. Wilson Biodiversity Foundation: www.eowbf.org
National Geographic Society: www.ngs.com
Public Broadcasting Service: www.pbs.org

Timelines:
International Commission on Stratigraphy (authority on geologic dates):
    www.stratigraphy.org
BBC Education/Evolution Website: www.bbc.co.uk/education/darwin/index.shtml
Enchanted Learning: www.enchantedlearning.com
History of the Universe: www.historyoftheuniverse.com
Palaeos: www.palaeos.com
Timelines of History: http://timelines.ws
The Tree of Life: http://tolweb.org/tree/phylogeny.html
University of Waikato, New Zealand/Timeline of Evolution: http://sci.waikato.ac.nz/
    evolution/EvolutionOfLife.shtml
Wikipedia: http://en.wikipedia.org/wiki/Timeline_of_evolution

Online encyclopedias:
Encyclopaedia Britannica: www.britannica.com
Wikipedia: www.wikipedia.org

MUSEUMS, AQUARIUMS, AND COLLECTIONS

Academy of Natural Sciences, Philadelphia, PA: www.acnatsci.org
American Museum of Natural History, New York, NY: www.amnh.org
The Australian Museum, Sydney, Australia: www.austmus.gov.au
California Academy of Sciences, San Francisco, CA: www.calacademy.org
Cambridge University Museum of Zoology, Cambridge, England: www.cam.ac.uk
Carnegie Museum of Natural History, Pittsburgh, PA: www.carnegiemnh.org
Denver Museum of Natural History, CO: www.dmnh.org
The Field Museum, Chicago, IL: www.fieldmuseum.org
Florence Museum of Natural History, Florence, Italy: www.unifi.it/unifi/msn
Harvard Museum of Natural History, Cambridge, MA: www.hmnh.harvard.edu
Houston Museum of Natural Science, Houston, TX: www.hmns.org
Marine Biological Laboratory, Woods Hole, MA: www.mbl.edu
Missouri Botanical Garden, St. Louis, MO: www.mobot.org
Monterey Bay Aquarium, Monterey, CA: www.mbayaq.org
Museo Nacional de Ciencias Naturales, Madrid, Spain: www.mncn.csic.es
Museum für Naturkunde, Berlin, Germany: www.museum.hu-berlin.de
Museum Mensch und Natur, Munich, Germany: www.musmn.de
Museum of New Zealand Te Papa Tongarewa, Wellington, New Zealand:
        www.tepapa.govt.nz
Museum of Science, Boston, MA: www.mos.org
Museum of the Earth, Ithaca, NY: www.museumoftheearth.org
Muséum National d'Histoire Naturelle, Paris, France: www.mnhn.fr
National Museum of Kenya, Nairobi, Kenya: www.museums.or.ke
Natural History Museum, London, England: www.nhm.ac.uk
Naturalis, the National Museum of Natural History, Leiden, Netherlands: www.naturalis.nl
Natur Historisches Museum, Vienna, Austria: www.nhm-wien.ac.at
Oxford University Museum of Natural History, Oxford, England: www.nhm.ac.uk
Peabody Museum of Natural History, New Haven, CT: www.peabody.yale.edu
Royal Botanic Gardens, Kew, Surrey, England: www.rbgkew.org.uk
Royal Tyrrell Museum of Paleontology, Alberta, Canada: www.tyrrellmuseum.com
Science Museum, Tokyo, Japan: www.jsf.or.jp
Smithsonian National Museum of Natural History, Washington, DC: www.mnh.si.edu
South African National Biodiversity Institute and the Kirstenbosch Botanical Garden, Cape
        Town, South Africa: www.nbi.ac.za
Swedish Museum of Natural History, Stockholm, Sweden: www.nrm.se
Sydney Aquarium, Sydney, Australia: www.sydneyaquarium.com.au
University of California at Berkeley Museum of Paleontology, Berkeley, CA:
        www.ucmp.berkeley.edu
University of Nebraska State Museum: www.explore-evolution.unl.edu
Vancouver Aquarium, Vancouver, Canada: www.vanaqua.org
Western Australian Museum, Perth, Australia: www.museum.wa.gov.au

C O N S E R V A T I O N

BirdLife International, Cambridge, England: www.birdlife.org
Conservation International, Washington, DC: www.conservation.org
Flora and Fauna International, Cambridge, England: www.flora-fauna.org
Frankfurt Zoological Society, Frankfurt, Germany: www.zgf.de
Nature Environment France: www.fne.asso.fr
Oceana, Washington, DC: www.oceana.org
The Nature Conservancy, Arlington, VA: www.nature.org
Wildlife Conservation Society, Bronx, NY: www.wcs.org
World Conservation Union, Gland, Switzerland: www.iucn.org
World Wildlife Fund USA, Washington, DC: www.worldwildlife.org
WWF-France, Paris, France: www.wwf.fr
WWF-Germany, Frankfurt, Germany: www.wwf.de
WWF-International, Gland, Switzerland: www.panda.org
WWF-Netherlands, Zeist, Netherlands: www.wnf.nl
WWF-Spain, Madrid, Spain: www.wwf.es

P H O T O G R A P H I C

All images for The Life Project were made with 35mm Nikon cameras. Film originals were scanned on Tango drum scanners. Both film and digital images were processed on Apple Power Mac G5 computers using Adobe Photoshop to prime them for reproduction. Epson professional inkjet printers were used to generate master proofs. The links below offer more information about photographic resources and technical support.

Nikon USA: www.nikonusa.com
Nikon Europe: www.europe-nikon.com

Professional Support: www.nikonpro.com
Digital Products and Information: www.nikondigital.com
Photographers and Images: www.nikonnet.com

Scanning: Colorfolio, www.colorfolio.com
Printers: Epson, www.epson.com
Printing Services: Calypso, www.calypsoinc.com
Camera Accessories: Really Right Stuff, www.reallyrightstuff.com
Filters: Singh-Ray, www.singh-ray.com
Underwater Camera Housings: Light and Motion Industries, www.lightandmotion.com
Underwater Photo Gear: Backscatter, www.backscatter.com
Photo Packs: Lowepro, www.lowepro.com; Tamrac, www.tamrac.com

A more detailed list of photographic resources and equipment used by Frans Lanting is featured at www.lanting.com/phototips_resources.html.

THE LIFE PROJECT is a lyrical interpretation of life on Earth from its earliest beginnings to its present diversity. In addition to this book, it includes a multimedia orchestral performance, a traveling photographic exhibition, and an educational website.

The multimedia version of *Life: A Journey Through Time*, with music for orchestra by Philip Glass, is produced by the Cabrillo Festival of Contemporary Music, led by music director and conductor Marin Alsop. After its premiere in the summer of 2006 in Santa Cruz, California, additional performances are planned in other cities in North America and Europe.

Life: A Journey Through Time is presented as a photographic exhibition by Naturalis, the National Museum of Natural History of the Netherlands. After its launch in the fall of 2006 in Leiden, the Netherlands, the exhibition is scheduled to tour through Europe and around the world.

A dedicated website, **www.LifeThroughTime.com**, serves as a portal for the project and as a source of information about the history of life on Earth. It connects viewers with images, stories, and links, and provides details about dates for musical performances, exhibits, presentations, and other events.

BIBLIOGRAPHY

Attenborough, David. *Life on Earth*. Little, Brown, 1979.

Ball, Philip. *The Self-made Tapestry: Pattern Formation in Nature*. Oxford University Press, 1999.

Ball, Philip. *Life's Matrix: A Biography of Water*. University of California Press, 2001.

Beard, Chris. *The Hunt for the Dawn Monkey*. University of California Press, 2004.

Briggs, John. *Fractals: The Patterns of Chaos*. Simon and Schuster, 1992.

Burnett, Nancy and Brad Matsen. *The Shape of Life*. Monterey Bay Aquarium Press, 2002.

Colbert, Edwin H. *Wandering Lands and Animals: The Story of Continental Drift and Animal Populations*. Dover Publications, 1985.

Cowen, Richard. *History of Life*. Blackwell Science, 2000.

Darling, David. *Life Everywhere: The Maverick Science of Astrobiology*. Basic Books, 2001.

Darwin, Charles. *On the Origin of Species*. John Murray, 1859.

Dawkins, Richard. *The Blind Watchmaker*. W. W. Norton, 1986.

Dawkins, Richard. *The Ancestor's Tale*. Houghton Mifflin, 2004.

Dawkins, Richard. *Climbing Mount Improbable*. W. W. Norton, 1996.

Diamond, Jared M. *The Third Chimpanzee*. HarperCollins, 1992.

Eldridge, Niles. *The Pattern of Evolution*. W. H. Freeman, 1999.

Eiseley, Loren. *The Immense Journey*. Random House, 1946.

Erwin, D. H. *Extinction: How Life on Earth Nearly Ended 250 Million Years Ago*. Princeton University Press, 2006.

Fenton, Carroll Lane, Mildred Adams Fenton, Patricia Vickers Rich, and Thomas Hewitt Rich. *The Fossil Book: A Record of Prehistoric Life*. Dover Publications, 1996.

Flannery, Tim. *The Future Eaters*. Reed Books, 1994.

Flannery, Tim. *The Eternal Frontier*. Grove Press, 2001.

Fortey, Richard. *Life: An Unauthorized Biography*. Alfred A. Knopf, 1997.

Fortey, Richard. *Trilobite: Eyewitness to Evolution*. Alfred A. Knopf, 2000.

Gould, Stephen Jay. *Wonderful Life*. W. W. Norton, 1989.

Gould, Stephen Jay. *The Book of Life*. W. W. Norton, 1993.

Haas, Ernst. *The Creation*. Viking Press, 1970.

Knoll, Andrew. *Life on a Young Planet*. Princeton University Press, 2003.

Lane, Nick. *Oxygen: The Molecule that made the World*. Oxford University Press, 2002.

Lovelock, James. *Gaia, A New Look at Life on Earth*. Oxford University Press, 1979.

Lovelock, James. *Homage to Gaia*. Oxford University Press, 2000.

Lovelock, James. *The Ages of Gaia, A Biography of Our Living Earth*. W. W. Norton, 1988.

Macdonald, David. *The Velvet Claw: A Natural History of the Carnivores*. BBC Books, 1992.

Margulis, Lynn. *Symbiotic Planet*. Basic Books, 1998.

Margulis, Lynn and Dorion Sagan. *Microcosmos: Four Billion Years of Microbial Evolution*. University of California Press, 1986.

Margulis, Lynn and Dorion Sagan. *Slanted Truths: Essays on Gaia, Symbiosis and Evolution.* Copernicus, 1997.

Margulis, Lynn and Dorion Sagan. *What is Life?* University of California Press, 1995.

Margulis, Lynn and Karlene V. Schwartz. *Five Kingdoms.* W. H. Freeman, 2001.

Martin, Paul. *Twilight of the Mammoths.* University of California Press, 2005.

Martin, Paul and H. Wright. *Pleistocene Extinctions: The Search for a Cause.* Yale University Press, 1967.

Mayr, Ernst. *Evolution and the Diversity of Life.* Harvard University Press, 1976.

McPhee, John. *Annals of the Former World.* Farrar, Straus and Giroux, 1998.

Morrison, Reg. *Australia: Land Beyond Time.* Cornell University Press, 2002.

Page, Barbara. *Rock of Ages, Sands of Time.* University of Chicago Press, 2001.

Parker, Andrew. *In the Blink of an Eye.* Free Press, 2003.

Quammen, David. *The Song of the Dodo: Island Biogeography in an Age of Extinctions.* Scribner, 1996.

Sagan, Carl. *Cosmos.* Random House, 1980.

Schopf, J. William. *Cradle of Life.* Princeton University Press, 1999.

Smil, Vaclav. *The Earth's Biosphere.* Massachusetts Institute of Technology, 2002.

Spinar, Zdenek V. and Zdenek Burian. *Life Before Man.* Thames and Hudson, 1972.

Thomas, Lewis. *The Lives of a Cell.* Bantam Books, 1974.

Thompson, D'Arcy Wentworth. *On Growth and Form.* Cambridge University Press, 1942.

Tudge, Colin. *Variety of Life: A Survey and a Celebration of all the Creatures that Have Ever Lived.* Oxford University Press, 2000.

Turney, Jon. *Lovelock and Gaia: Signs of Life.* Columbia University Press, 2003.

Vernadsky, Vladimir. *The Biosphere.* Springer-Verlag, 1997.

Walker, Gabrielle. *Snowball Earth.* Three Rivers Press, 2003.

Ward, Peter Douglas. *The Call of Distant Mammoths.* Copernicus, 1997.

Ward, Peter Douglas. *On Methuselah's Trail: Living Fossils and the Great Extinctions.* W. H. Freeman, 1992.

Ward, Peter D. and Donald Brownlee. *The Life and Death of Planet Earth.* Times Books, 2002.

Wegener, Alfred. *The Origin of Continents and Oceans.* Dover Publications, 1966.

White, Mary E. *Earth Alive! From Microbes to a Living Planet.* Rosenberg, 2003.

White, Mary E. *The Flowering of Gondwana.* Princeton University Press, 1990.

Wilson, Edward O. *The Diversity of Life.* Harvard University Press, 1992.

Woese, Carl. "Bacterial evolution," *Microbiological Reviews* 51:221-271, 1987.

ACKNOWLEDGMENTS

This book is a synthesis of research and fieldwork on all seven continents over a period of many years. When I think of the people and institutions who have supported my efforts in one way or another I feel gratitude for the knowledge, the trust, the hospitality, and the friendship that has been extended to me over the years. Thank you all.

ON LOCATION :

A F R I C A Botswana: Ralph Bousfield, David Dugmore, Mike Gunn, Lloyd Wilmot; Botswana Department of Wildlife and National Parks. **Congo Basin:** Takeshi Furuichi, Takayoshi Kano. **Kenya and Tanzania:** Karl Ammann, Steve Turner. **Madagascar:** Steve Goodman, Alison Jolly, Olivier Langrand, Martin Nicoll, Eckehart Olszowski, Jean-Paul Paddack, Hubert Randrianasolo, Alison Richard. **Namibia:** Wayne and Lise Hanssen, Laurie Marker. **South Africa:** Bruce Anderson, Phil Desmet, Allen Ellis, Kristal Maze, Ernst van Jaarsveld; Kirstenbosch Botanical Garden.

A N T A R C T I C A A N D T H E S O U T H E R N O C E A N Antarctica: At Wilderness Travel: Bill Abbott, Ray Rodney, and staff; at Zegrahm Expeditions: Peter Harrison, Mike Messick, Werner Zehnder and staff. **The Falklands:** Tony Chater, the Poncet family.

A S I A A N D T H E P A C I F I C Hawaii: Brad and Annabelle Lewis, David Okita; at the National Park Service: Jim Gale, Mardie Lane; at the Hawaii Volcano Observatory: Jenda Johnson, Jim Kauahikaua, Grant Kaye, Tim Orr, Don Swanson; at the U. S. Fish and Wildlife Service: Jack Jeffrey. **Borneo/Malaysia:** Steve Pinfield, Noel Richard; Danum Valley Field Centre. **Mongolia:** Inge Bouman and the Foundation Reserves Przewalski Horse, Puujee Jachin, the late Jachin Tserendeleg; Hustain Nuruu National Park. **Kamchatka/Russia:** Vera Dmitrieva, Gennadi Karpov, Anna-Louise Reysenbach, Karl Stetter.

A U S T R A L I A A N D N E W Z E A L A N D Australia: David Bettini, Peter Cooper, the late Jean-Paul Ferrero, Tim Flannery, Mike Gillam, Kath Grey, John Horniblow, Vere Kenny, Peter Kopke, Helen Larson, Bruce Munday, Jonathan Munro, Graham Phelps, Phil Playford, Joel Simon, Richard and Lyn Woldendorp; at the Australian Museum: Carl Bento; at the Sydney Aquarium: Paul Eagar. **New Zealand:** Alison Ballance, Andrew Buttle, Gideon Climo, Charles Daugherty, Libby Fletcher, Paddy Follas, Arno Gasteiger, Richard Holdaway, Harvey James, Alastair Jamieson, Matt McGlone, Nicola Mitchell, Rod Morris, Brad Scott, Jean-Claude Stahl, Kennedy Warne; at the Department of Conservation: Andy Blick, Wayne Costello, Daryl Eason, Graeme Elliott, Paul Jansen, Greg Lind, Pete McClelland, Don Merton.

C E N T R A L A N D S O U T H A M E R I C A Belize: Tony Rath; at the Belize Zoo: Sharon Matola. **Brazil:** Paulo Boute, Ary Soares, Casey Westbrook. **Costa Rica:** Michael and Patricia Fogden. **Galápagos:** Godfrey Merlen and Gayle Davis-Merlen; Charles Darwin Research Station, Galápagos National Park Service. **Peru:** Charles Munn and Mariana Valqui Munn, Eduardo Nycander and the staff at Tambopata Research Center, Tom Schulenberg, John Terborgh. **Surinam:** Frans Buissink, Henk and Judy Reichart; Stinasu.

EUROPE AND NORTH AMERICA Canada: Vancouver Aquarium.
Finland: Hannu and Irma Hautala, Matti Torkkomaki. **Netherlands:** G. A. C. Veeneman
and the staff at the Museum Boerhaave, Leiden. **USA: Alaska:** Kelly and Natalie Bay,
Paul and Donna Claus, Neil Darish, Gary Green, John Tucker. **Arizona:** Dick Carter.
California: Alex and Sybilla Balkanski, Jim Cheatham, Stephen Sharnoff; at the Agouron
Institute: Joan Kobori, Mel Simon; at the California Academy of Sciences: the late Luis
Baptista, John McCosker; at Diversa: Paula Devereux, Martin Keller, Ed Shonsey; at Long
Marine Lab: Steve Davenport, Gary Griggs; at the Monterey Bay Aquarium: Julie Packard,
Ken Peterson, Bruce Upton; at the Orchid Zone: Terry Root; at Sonoma State University:
Nicholas Geist; at the University of California: Lynda Goff, MRC Greenwood; at the
University of California Los Angeles: Jared Diamond; at the University of California
Santa Cruz: Dan Costa, Ken Doctor, Dan Harder, Burney LeBoeuf, Scott Shaffer, and
John Thompson. **Colorado:** Steve Hess. **Florida:** At the Marie Selby Botanical Garden:
Bruce Holst. **Georgia:** At Emory University: Frans de Waal. **Illinois:** At the University of
Illinois: Bruce Fouke. **Massachusetts:** At Harvard University's Farlow Herbarium: Robert
Edgar; at MIT: John Grotzinger; at the University of Massachusetts: Lynn Margulis; at the
Woods Hole Marine Biological Laboratory: Robert Barlow. **Missouri:** At the Missouri
Botanical Garden: Peter Raven, Alan Graham. **New York:** At the American Museum of
Natural History: Joel Cracraft, Niles Eldridge. **Pennsylvania:** At Pennsylvania State
University: James Kasting. **Utah:** Ken Brown, Paul Swanstrom. **Washington:** Dale
Huett; at the University of Washington: Peter Douglas Ward; **Washington, DC:** At the
National Museum of Health and Medicine: William Discher, Elizabeth Lockett.

PROFESSIONAL SUPPORT

Many of the photographs in this book were produced in the course of assignments for
which I would like to thank the original sponsors. Others were made possible by the
professional and technical expertise of the people and organizations mentioned below.
My sincere thanks to Nikon for providing equipment and support for The Life Project.
Special thanks are due to the National Geographic Society for the opportunities, the
resources, and the trust that enabled me to create images that would not have been
possible otherwise.

National Geographic Society: Terry Adamson, Keith Bellows, Melina Gerosa Bellows,
Bob Booth, Dennis Dimick, Bill Douthitt, John Fahey, Bert Fox, John Francis, Terry Garcia,
David Griffin, John Griffin, Chris Johns, Bill Marr, Glynnis McPhee, Kathy Moran, Susan
Norton, Sadie Quarrier, Susan Smith, and Ellen Stanley; Larry Maurer, Joe Stancampiano,
Kenji Yamaguchi, and the staff at Photo Engineering; and former colleagues John Agnone,
Bill Allen, Rich Clarkson, Bill Garrett, Bob Gilka, Tom Kennedy, and Mary Smith. **GEO:**
Christiane Breustedt, Ruth Eichhorn, Peter-Mathias Gaede, Venita Kaleps. **Nikon Europe:**
Martina Beckmann. **Nikon USA:** Anna-Marie Bakker, Mike Corrado, Ed Fasano, Steve
Heiner, Bo Kajiwara, and Joe Ventura; Nikon Professional Services. At Backscatter:
Berkley White; at Light and Motion Industries: Dan Baldocchi; at Really Right Stuff: Joe
Johnson; at Singh-Ray: Bob Singh.

ACKNOWLEDGMENTS

SPECIAL THANKS for help with the realization of The Life Project go to: At the Blue Earth Alliance: Natalie Fobes, Adam Weintraub, and staff; at the Cabrillo Festival of Contemporary Music: Marin Alsop, Ellen Primack, Nancy Bertossa, Tom Fredericks, and Nancy Loshkajian; and for the multimedia orchestral performance of *Life*: Peter Coyote, Alex Nichols, and Philip Glass; at Calypso: Joe and Barbara Levine; at the E. O. Wilson Biodiversity Foundation: Jay Short, Leif Christoffersen, and Eric Mathur; at Gilholm Productions: Greg Gilholm; at Harvard University: Andrew Knoll; at Naturalis: Peter Aartsen, Dirk Houtgraaf, Lars van den Hoek Ostende, Sjan Janssen, Frank Wesselingh, Peter Zuure; at the Smithsonian: Louise Emmons, Douglas Erwin; at Swat Team Partners: Randy Antik; at the TED Conference: Chris Anderson; at Teleportec: Jim and Carole Young; at Thinc Design: Tom Hennes, Linus Lam; Patrick Zimmerli; at the University of California Santa Cruz: David Deamer; at Xplore: Peter Heres; and to friends Lauralee Alben, Wade Davis and Gail Percy, Kathryn Fuller, Caroline Getty, Rob and Myrna Lindeman, David and Stephanie Mills, and Bob and Judy Waterman. I bow to Reg Morrison, a fellow time traveler who showed me the way, and to the late Ernst Haas, whose images in his book *The Creation* inspired me to adopt photography as a language and as a way to interpret the world. Humble thanks go to the authors listed in the bibliography, whose work and words helped me understand the story of life.

SINCERE APPRECIATION for assistance with the making of this book go to: Ted Benhari and Karla Hutton, Michael DeLapa, Peter Doven, Jennie Dusheck, Isabel Stirling, and our Florida "tech team," Paul and Betty Eckstrom. At the Frans Lanting Studio: Erica Allen, Debbie Hickey, Audra McKay, Yann Nicolas, Doug Niven, Neil Osborne, and Mary Salazar; at Taschen: Florian Kobler and Frank Goerhardt, Thomas Grell, Barbara Huttrop, Kora Krines, Pedro Lisboa, Jason Mitchell, Kathrin Murr, Horst Neuzner, Rüdiger Tiedemann, Christine Waiblinger, Veronica Weller, and Nina Wiener; and to Kristen Wurz for her fine layout production. A very special thank you goes to Bob Cornelis of Colorfolio, and Bill Atkinson, who generously created the superb scans of the images featured in this book.

A personal word of appreciation goes to Benedikt Taschen for the gift of creative freedom; to Jennifer Barry for her elegant design and guidance; and to Jane Vessels for her excellent editorial judgment.

To Chris Eckstrom goes my eternal gratitude for joining me and enriching the journey of life.

Produced by Frans Lanting and Christine Eckstrom in association
with TASCHEN

Copyright © 2006 Terra Editions, a division of Frans Lanting Productions
www.lanting.com

Photographs and Text © 2006 Frans Lanting, Santa Cruz, California

Editor: Christine Eckstrom, Santa Cruz, California

Design: Jennifer Barry Design, Fairfax, California

Published by TASCHEN GmbH,
Hohenzollernring 53, 50672 Cologne, Germany
www.taschen.com

Editorial Coordination: Florian Kobler, Cologne
Production: Frank Goerhardt and Thomas Grell, Cologne

Images from this book are available for licensing through the Frans Lanting
Image Collection, www.franslanting.com; email: photo@lanting.com.

Fine prints and collector's editions of Frans Lanting's books are available
through the Frans Lanting Gallery, www.lanting.com; email: gallery@lanting.com.

To stay informed about new TASCHEN titles, please request a magazine at
www.taschen.com/magazine or write to: TASCHEN America, 6671 Sunset Boulevard,
Suite 1508, Los Angeles, CA 90028 USA; email: contact-us@taschen.com.
Fax: +1-323-463.4442. We will be happy to send you a free copy of our magazine which is
filled with information about all of our books.

ISBN-13: 978-3-8228-3994-2
ISBN-10: 3-8228-3994-9

Printed in Italy

FOLLOWING PAGE:
PAGE 304: Human Brain

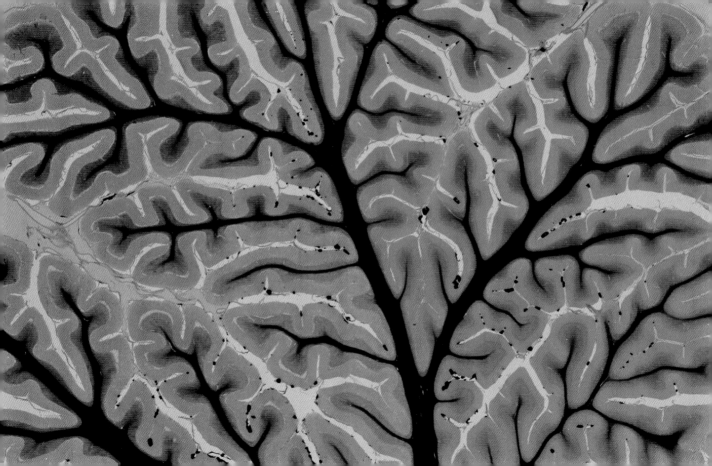